Assuming the Position

A Memoir of Hustling

by Rick Whitaker

D0065141

FOUR WALLS EIGHT WINDOWS
NEW YORK/LONDON

Published in the United States by
Four Walls Eight Windows
39 West 14th Street
New York, NY 10011
http://www.fourwallseightwindows.com

UK offices:
Four Walls Eight Windows/Turnaround
Unit 3 Olympia Trading Estate
Coburg Road, Wood Green
London N22 67Z

First printing September 1999.

Library of Congress Cataloging-in-Publication Data:
Whitaker, Rick, 1968–   Assuming the position: a memoir of
hustling / by Rick Whitaker.   p. cm. ISBN 1-56858-123-8 (cloth)
1. Whitaker, Rick, 1968–   . 2. Male prostitutes—New York
(State)—New York Biography. 3. Gay men—New York (State)—
New York—Biography. 4. Male prostitution—New York (State)—
New York. I. Title. HQ146.N7W45   1999   306.74'3'092—dc21 [B]
99-33495 CIP

Text design and composition by Ink, Inc., New York.
Printed in the United States

10 9 8 7 6 5 4

For Paul Kellogg

How evil it is to buy Love, and how evil to sell it! And yet what purple hours one can snatch from that grey slowly-moving thing we call Time! . . . The Cloister or the Café— there is my future. I tried the Hearth, but it was a failure.

—Oscar Wilde

The façade tends with most people, I suppose, as the years go by, to grow inward so that what began as a protection and screen of the naked soul becomes itself the soul.

—Leonard Woolf

ASSUMING THE POSITION

1.

The first time I worked as a prostitute, I went to Rounds, a bar on the East Side well known for its clientele of hustlers and johns. I had, at the time, a rather dubious motive aside from a real but customary need for money. My boyfriend, Tom, was leaving me, and I knew he had hustled in the past. I was in love with Tom and I wanted, I guess, to experience something intense that he had gone through, vaguely expecting that it would help me to understand him better and that it might even somehow bring us back together when he found out about it. I don't really know how I rationalized this at the time, and perhaps I just did it without justification, but hustling seemed like an extreme measure commensurate with the power of my passion for Tom. If he was going to leave me, I was going to become a hustler, saluting him, as it were, with a crude gesture I hoped he would recognize as desperate.

I was nervous about the whole thing. I didn't know, to begin with, if I was attractive enough to get work. But once inside the bar I relaxed a little when I saw that there was an easy, erotic feel to the place and that I was about as young and good-looking as anyone else there. I was twenty-five. I was prepared for a room full of nine-teen-year-old model types and gorgeously dangerous kids, but that is not what I found. There was a wide variety of hustlers at this famous bar—from young black boys up from Christopher Street to forty-year-old veterans with big dicks and enormous muscles. There were straight guys who made good money letting the queers suck them off, and there were prissy gay boys looking for "security." Some of the hustlers looked a little sweaty and rough, and I would have been glad to pay a few of them for the good fuck they appeared to promise if I'd had the money. Several times that night I was unsure about whether someone was buying or selling, and I didn't know how to respond to attention from a man five or six years older than me who seemed just to want free sex. I was also unclear about how to negotiate a deal; but I had another drink and watched for a while, and before long a deal had been made.

George was an overweight and balding lawyer, but he looked clean and trustworthy, and he appeared to have taken quite a liking to me. I was flattered by his exclusive interest: he seemed to have found exactly what he wanted. About fifteen minutes and a martini later, when he suggested taking a taxi with him to

Brooklyn and paying me $150 plus taxi fare back to Manhattan, I agreed.

It was a long ride to George's apartment in a neighborhood the name of which I never knew. He lived in an enormous, ugly building with a depressing little fountain in front that was lit by scrawny colored lights. His apartment was furnished in a way I have come to associate generally with johns. The furniture is always about five or ten or fifteen years old—not new and not old. There is a large, low table in front of the sofa, usually made of glass or clear plastic or something painted white, upon which rest neat piles of magazines and a big glass ashtray. The whole apartment is carpeted, and there are full-length mirrors at several corners of the living room. The tall halogen lamps are brightly lit. The decor and mood feel a little forced, as if the man who lives in this organized place is determined to be comfortable there. The bedroom has more mirrors, and the bed is covered by an acrylic, floral-pattern blanket. The windows are never open; the room is air-conditioned all summer, which the man considers an indispensable luxury. The whole place is bleak in a completely ordinary way.

And George, like many of my clients, had a dog, which he seemed a little embarrassed to talk to in my presence, as if he believed he usually talked to the dog rather too much.

I was naturally ignorant about exactly how to behave on my first evening as a prostitute. I was prepared to be afraid of murder, rape, and satanic gang bangs, but George's building was so middle-class that I couldn't imagine anything happening there that a scream for help wouldn't bring to a quick and embarrassing end, and George seemed anything but dangerous. He turned out to have few expectations, and it was not at all difficult to make him happy. The very fact that he had hired a young man to come home with him was exciting for George, and I responded to his excitement. Before long I was standing up on his bed fucking his mouth, encouraging him madly. I surprised myself—though I didn't, I think, surprise George. He seemed prepared for everything that happened and ended up having what looked like a wholesome, cathartic orgasm. Afterward I made a point of lounging voluptuously on his brown velour sofa, sipping a Coca-Cola, making sure to give George his money's worth right up to the moment of walking out the door an hour after I'd arrived.

He called a taxi for me, and when I left I suddenly felt very sad. I was feeling George's sadness—which for all I know he wasn't even feeling himself—in addition to my own. George's money was a lump in my pocket. I felt that I had reminded a lonely man of his loneliness and then left him to it. I thought George should not have done what he did and that I should not have taken advantage of his weakness.

I was probably wrong to feel this way. In fact, George (who was a lawyer, after all) probably had no trouble paying my fee, and if he was lonely at midnight, at least he was less lonely at ten, when he'd been with me. He was capable, with me, of some sexy behavior that I suspect he found pretty impressive. George did not strike me as a person with a great deal of self-confidence, but he was surely suffering no lack of conviction when he was sucking my cock. At the time, though, I could only feel that what George and I had done together was depressing and disheartening, and on some level it was.

Back in Manhattan I phoned Tom, the ex-boyfriend, from a pay phone, in tears, and told him about what I'd done. He reproached me brusquely and told me not to do it again, which compelled me to do it again the very next night. Over the next few weeks I committed myself to what was then, for me, a neurotic, sacrificial activity, trying to ease the hurt of having been abandoned by doing something I hoped would hurt Tom. I wanted to be scarred by experience and able thereby to show that my love for him was potent and real. I don't think my hustling hurt Tom much, and in any event we never got back together. I am still, in a way, in love with him, though I don't believe that is why I continued for so long to prostitute myself.

☙

I remember Rounds, the bar, as a bizarre, somewhat wicked place. I liked it. I met all sorts of people there, including an older man who, according to rumor, hired every one of the hustlers that passed through the place and was equally passionate and demanding with all of them. He took me to a cheap hotel in the East Thirties where I remember not a word passed between him and the Asian man behind the fluorescent-lit counter; the little man just handed my client a key and we went up to a gloomy, windowless room with a bed in it. From the very beginning of the evening, this guy had been making me promise I would see him again the next day, and that I would allow him to "take care of me." I was to be his "nephew," and he would be my "uncle." I told him that I did not often have sex with my uncles, and he told me not to think about it like that. We won't be "having sex," he said, we'll just make each other feel good. Everything this man said to me, I believe, was a lie; his was my first encounter with the kind of prolific dissembling that often serves to lubricate and justify for himself a john's experience with a hustler. Most of the men who hired me, unlike George, the lawyer from Brooklyn, seemed unable or unwilling to accept the simplicity of having hired a young man to come over and have sex with them. It was as if that was not interesting enough for them—there had to be some psychodrama involved in addition to the sex for them to get their money's worth.

Anyway, my "uncle" turned out to have some pretty energetic ideas about "making me feel good" and vice versa. His modus operandi, I learned later from another hustler at Rounds, was to seek out the most inexperienced hustler, coo to him about how good he will be to him and how much money he will give him over time, and then to get the boy into that dreary hotel and get as much sex out of him as he could for the least amount of money the kid would accept. Working out of the bar—unlike working for an agency, which I did later—there were no real rules, and negotiations were

usually over a price and little more. Most clients expect
no more than an hour of a hustler's time. But then most
people are reasonable, and some just aren't. My "uncle"
that night used what he worked up as our affection for
each other—our fledgling friendship—to persuade me
to stay with him long into the night. He was not at all
reluctant to tell me how lonely he was, and how desperately he needed me to stay with him. He said he
would give me money every day if I would be his
"nephew." And then he would suck my dick again or
ask for another "massage." I do not resent much of what
I went through in my years as a hustler, but I am sorry
that so early in my career I encountered the kind of
emotional pleading this repellent man used to his
advantage. He was a real nuisance, and I have never
been able quite to forget the intensity of his undisci-
plined, unscrupulous need.

I did occasionally pick up another hustler at Rounds
for fun. Usually we would plan to meet at a bar downtown at about 2:00 A.M., after we'd both made some
money. Then we would share some coke to wake ourselves up, have a couple of drinks, and go someplace to
fuck. Sometimes one of us had more work than we
expected and couldn't make the appointment at the bar

on time, and, in any case, hustlers tend not to be punctual when they're not making money. It's a loose life, and the nights are long. Sex with other hustlers is best anyway when you're all getting paid for it. Some of the most picturesque sex I've ever had was on exhibition for paying customers. I remember one night at the Peninsula Hotel when a well-known restaurant owner had flown in his "friend" Chris from Los Angeles and hired me to join them. Chris was an Italian who loved nothing more than getting fucked by a hustler for hours, and the other guy liked nothing more than to watch. Since Chris happened to be very cute and about twenty-four years old, I was happy to oblige. The fact that we were being watched and paid only added to the excitement.

After a couple of weeks I quit going to Rounds. I had a part-time job and did not really need the money (though I certainly enjoyed having it), and I found the bar monotonous after a while. It was in a neighborhood not easily got to from where I lived, and it was more fun to go downtown. I lost interest in hustling; it was too much work. And it did not appear to be making any difference in my defunct relationship with Tom, who was by then (and still is) living happily with somebody else.

He cared about me, I believe, but he was not in love with me, and leaving me unequivocally was surely the right thing to do. Hustling out of the bar had been a way to distract myself from feeling hurt about Tom, because I could feel hurt by men more generally that way—hurt, in fact, it seemed, by the world, which was easier somehow than being hurt so intensely by Tom. If my life had led me to working as a hustler in a bar, okay; I could accept *that* kind of a tragedy because it was not, or did not seem to be, personal. It was a cultural tragedy.

Rounds was eventually closed down and became another old legend—people swear that Tom Cruise once bartended there. I had nothing to do with hustling for a while. I had my part-time job and I proofread books on the side, and I was close to finishing my undergraduate degree. I was writing reviews and a novel, and looking, a little heartbrokenly, for a new boyfriend. I had some good friends, thank god, and I liked my life.

I finished the degree (in philosophy) and I finished the novel, and then I screwed up a proofreading job and couldn't get freelance work from Random House anymore. I found an agent for the novel, but she was unable to get it published. The idea of taking a full-time job was identical, for me, to admitting failure as a writer, which I was not prepared to do. I began to get a little hopeless. I didn't find a boyfriend—no one resisted me the way Tom had, and no one was, partly for that reason, as interesting.

Disappointed by the meager rewards of hard work, I began to believe that hedonism was as good a philosophy as any, and better than most. If nothing matters, then why not have a good time while I can? I drank a lot and allowed myself to experiment more with drugs than I had before, and I had a great deal of sex with strangers, some of it unsafe. The hours I kept began to exclude, for the most part, daytime.

I decided one day about a year after my last misadventure at Rounds to look into hustling again. I needed money, and hustling was appealing because it was lucrative, it was against the law, and it was congruent with what was by then my fairly serious drug habit. I snorted cocaine almost nightly, smoked a lot of pot, and occasionally snorted heroin. I also took lots of pills and got drunk every night. I have always admired stylish outlaws of all sorts, and my drug use together with a good deal of shoplifting already gave me a private status I liked; earning my living by means outside the law seemed at the time like something I wanted to try. It still has a certain appeal, I must admit.

I called up the number for an escort agency I'd found on a printed ad, and after responding to a couple of simple questions (such as, Have you done this kind of work before? to which I replied, Well, I understand what kind of work it is), I agreed to come in for an interview, where, I was told, I would be expected briefly to remove my clothes.

I arrived precisely on time since the agent had asked me not to be early. I waited a few minutes on a red upholstered chair, overhearing the owner speaking to a client on the telephone and his colleague interviewing another aspiring escort in the adjacent room. The owner was saying into the phone, Tell me, what kind of men do you like?... Of *course* I could send over a black man! James is twenty-four, six-two, *principally* a top, very nice. He's an *athlete*.... Would *I* be sending him to you if he was *dangerous?* The owner sat before a small, elaborate desk; I could see on the desk only index cards, pens, and fifty- and hundred-dollar bills. He was wearing tight shorts and a tank top, and everything he said was in a surprising tone—it was more aggressive, or more tender, or nostalgic, or surprised than I would have expected, as if things had an eccentric meaning for him.

The interview in the next room did not seem to be

going well. The interviewee was very shy and self-effacing, and the other man sounded frustrated and slightly mocking.

During my interview with the owner's colleague—a large, rather ugly man in his late forties—we frankly discussed my versatility and experience. I said that I was sexually versatile, but could not agree to do everything with everyone: I'd fuck a man I found attractive, and on a good night I might let such a man fuck me, but I couldn't promise to get a hard-on for a man I didn't like. The man interviewing me said that no one expected me to get an erection at the drop of a hat; but would I let a paying customer suck my dick? Yes, I said, I suppose I would.

He told me how the business was run and the terms of the arrangement: my fee would be $250 per hour, of which the agency would get $100. I would be expected to bring them their money at the end of each job. Regular customers from years ago, when the rates were lower, were charged the old rate of $200, of which I would make only $100. How many of those are there? I asked. Not many, the man said. They're mostly dead. This was not encouraging, but I let it pass without much thought. Then I was asked to show the agent my body. I removed my shirt and then let down my pants. I was a little cold and more than a little nervous (and not at all aroused), so I was worried that the impression I made was, well, scant. But I was confident, I said, that under different circumstances my true endowment would make itself apparent, and I told the man that I had never had much in the way of complaints from lovers. The agent seemed to believe me and took down a measurement I was happy to accept. He and the owner, who joined us when I was nude, told me I was hired on the spot, and that I should buy a pager with the proceeds from my first call, which would turn out to take place that very night.

I left the bizarre apartment—lots of chandeliers and mirrors in the two small, brown rooms, and a dog in the kitchen—and went downtown, in the opposite direction from where I live. It was 8:45 P.M., and I didn't feel like going home. The interview had taken forty-five minutes: three times as long as they had said it would take, which I noted with some satisfaction. I felt they had liked me, and I was glad.

On the subway after the interview, I thought to myself that working for the agency would be very different from my experience at Rounds. The relationship that develops in a bar and subsequently on the taxi ride to the john's home or hotel is often loaded with the suggestion—as with my "uncle"—of a developing friendship and intimacy; thus the ugly feelings, at least on my part, when the little *amitié* comes to its abrupt, commercial termination. The mediation of an agency gives a more businesslike dynamic to the whole transaction. As in psychotherapy, both parties benefit from the structured time and the payment of a set fee. And the men who can afford the agency's "high-end" rates are generally less troubled by the expense.

I had something to eat, phoned my answering service (no messages), and went to my favorite East Village bar. I had a drink and found, to my surprise, that I had no interest in meeting anyone, or even in sex, if it wasn't going to add something to the nonsexual till. I felt arrogant, as if my services were too valuable to give away, which was a wonderfully empowering state of mind. This feeling would later contribute to my difficulty in sustaining sexual interest in men I was attracted to but not in love with. The arrogance eventually became a psychological burden, an unwanted defense. But at the time it felt pretty good. I was beholden to no one—that's how I felt. I couldn't be rejected because I wasn't available, except for a price too high for the guys in that place to afford. I had no desire. Normally my lust for company makes me vulnerable. But that night I was untouchable, maybe for the first time in my life. Someone casually said to me once that anybody can be a hustler. But any hustler knows that's not true, and that night I knew that I had the looks, the courage, the recklessness, and, now, the agency. I was ready for my new life.

I phoned my service again and found that the agent had rung. After a brief call to him, I nervously got into a taxi and headed for the Carlyle Hotel. The agent had told me that the client, a businessman from Texas, wanted to take me to the bar downstairs for a drink before going back up to his room, which was fine with me, though the agent didn't like the idea. He said it was a waste of time, and it turned out that he was right.

I was surprised by the ease with which I was able to walk through the lobby of the Carlyle and into the elevator with no questions asked at 11:00 at night. I suppose if I had been dressed less well, or arrived even later in the night, or was black, I might have been stopped. But I just went on up to a high floor of the hotel and knocked on the door. A red-faced man in his sixties answered and spoke to me in a moderate, soothing Texas accent, and we shook hands. I asked to use the toilet before going down to the bar, and while I was relieving myself, the Texan peeked in and politely asked me if he could watch. I agreed.

In the bar downstairs we sat at a corner table and John (I believe that was actually his name) put his hand on my knee, which I noticed that several people were able to observe. I thought it was strange that John did not mind being seen with me in this cozy, romantic public situation. He was married, he told me, and the agent had told me that he was very wealthy. He had children and was in New York for business. But I figured that if he wasn't afraid I had no real right to object, and I tried to enjoy the attention. John asked me what I did besides *this,* though he did not appear to be very interested when I proceeded to tell him about my background as a student of music and philosophy, my interest in writing, and my work in publishing. He told me about his wife and children, who were older than I. John was cheerful and a nice enough guy, though without a great deal of charm. He neither attracted nor frightened me. I felt indifferent about what was to come, and I was bored with chatting.

John asked me if I had condoms with me—the agent had told him I would. I didn't. I honestly explained that this was my first night working for an agency and I hadn't had time to stock up. I couldn't really imagine we were going to need any condoms, but I said I would go out and find some on my own time and come back as quickly as possible. John said he wanted to come with me, though, so he signed the check and we got into a taxi and found a deli a block away. I got out and paid for the condoms and we took the taxi around the block and went back into the hotel. John seemed almost proud to walk through the lobby with me at a few minutes past midnight.

That first night, especially after forgetting the condoms, I was very nervous and it showed. We did not have occasion to use the condoms we'd gone out for. I found it impossible to relax. I recall John lying on the hotel bed and me standing to the side trying in vain to bring my dick to life. John, I believe, wanted to give me a blow job, but he was not interested unless I could offer an erection, and I simply could not. He was wonderfully understanding and forgiving, and I did my very best to make the hour erotic somehow. I could sense that John was disappointed, but I believe that in the long run he got some degree of the pleasure he felt himself entitled to.

The work I did that first night for the agency was the most difficult of its kind that I have ever done. A relaxed atmosphere and a hard-on are certainly preferable to emotional tension and its physical repercussions, both for the client and the escort, but they can't be forced. I was uptight and I punished myself for it, which is not the way to achieve an erection. I was not at all attracted sexually to John, but in the subsequent months I learned how to make almost any situation with a client sexy by focusing on the fact that *he is* attracted to me. Eventually I would use the client's excitement to trick myself, or my body, into believing that a sexual response was appropriate. This capacity for deliberate self-delusion is at the heart of the whole matter: the way comfortably to take a new role is to make it a habit. But habits are hard to break. I was pleased with myself when I found that I had learned how to perform for my clients; I didn't reflect, at the time, on the consequences of this new facility. What I overlooked was the fact that I could no longer relate to people *at all* except in this new, assumed mode. Before long I had become a fake. I was good at it, and I liked it, and there are times now when I miss it. I was protected, as a hustler, by my invented self. Unfortunately, the invention was too simple to serve any but the most banal situations, so I began to avoid any but the most banal.

I spent just over two hours with John, including drinks and the trip to the deli. Before I left, he handed me slightly more than the fee for one hour and asked if that was all right, implying that an hour's fee was all I had really earned. I was too unsure of myself, then, to get the full fee for two hours. I did manage to say that the agency expected him to pay for all the time I had spent with him, and he turned over a little more money. What I had made, then, was not enough, but it was a lot. It was roughly equivalent to what I'd been making (and make now) for working two whole days. And it was tax free.

℘

I had assumed that hustling was dangerous, and no doubt some of it is. But I was never afraid of violence from a man an agency sent me to see, and I was never seriously hurt by any of them. (I have been hurt some-what by many of them: mostly my feelings were hurt, but occasionally I would get bitten hard or slapped, and once I got a sharp elbow to my nose, but that was an accident.) The men always paid me without complaint. I have wondered what would have happened if I had insisted on a full two-hour fee from John. Probably he

would have given it. We were, after all, in a room at the
Carlyle Hotel under his name, and I'm sure he would
not have wanted trouble. In this sense (and in others),
male prostitutes must have it much easier than their
female counterparts. I almost always sensed that clients
were at least potentially a little afraid of me, and I always
felt perfectly comfortable setting limits to our sexual
activities. An agent said to me once that I was paid for
my time, nothing more. This seemed an odd thing for an
agent to tell his employee, but it's true: I never did anything I wasn't willing and able to do. There were certainly times when I went to the edge, and did things that
I didn't know I would do, but that is altogether different
from being coerced. Usually, it's better to make the
client happy and be on your way. And you probably
shouldn't be working as an escort if you don't enjoy
many different kinds of sex.

Two weeks later I did two jobs within six hours. The
first was with an executive at his apartment in midtown.
He had a vinyl-upholstered sofa upon and around
which, it appeared, he lived his entire domestic life,
which consisted of drinking, smoking, reading popular
magazines, watching television, and listening to a dismal
collection of a dozen or so compact discs. He smoked

ultra-light menthol cigarettes and had a moustache. He
began to tell me about himself, about his job and his past.
I recall that he made his job sound unbearably dull, and
he confessed that he almost never left the neighborhood,
which was near Grand Central Station. He had had one
lover, and they had just split up a few months before. I
had been hired to begin the process of drawing him out
and persuading him that he was "still sexy." I could sense,
by then, the signs of too much friendliness, and I took
my shirt off in order to get things moving along in a
more sexual, less intimate way. I led him from the sofa
and after he tried for a while to fuck me, fumbling terribly with the condom, we gave that up and I brought him
eventually to orgasm. It wasn't easy, but it was work I was
competent to do, and it didn't seem too awful at the time.
I certainly was not attracted to this man, but it didn't matter so much as it had with John two weeks before,
because by now I had already become something of a
professional. I'd learned some mental tricks, and they
usually worked. (These tricks are not easily described.
They're combinations of fantasy, blindness, and a kind of
instinctive muting of emotions.) Afterward, I showered
in the executive's clean, plain bathroom, and he paid me,
with no tip.

I thought my work for the night was done, and went out for a drink (it immediately became a habit never to go directly home after working). At 12:30, my pager buzzed again in my pocket; it was the agent again, saying that he really needed me to do another job because this was a regular, wealthy client whom he tried to take especially good care of. And he was known sometimes to tip extremely well. I reluctantly agreed to go. Again I got into a taxi and went off to a ritzy hotel, this one on Central Park South, where the client lived.

I could hardly believe it when a young, handsome man answered the door. He was wearing a sumptuous terry cloth robe. I later found out that he was well known, first for his previous job in magazine publishing and now for his position working closely with a successful fashion designer, and for his good looks, wealth, and charm. I liked him, and we had some very good sex. He really did appear to live permanently in a medium-sized generic room in a very expensive hotel, which struck me as both luxurious and uncomfortable. After he paid me, with a generous tip, we talked for half an hour before I left. He was very interested to hear about the novel I was writing, and we discussed some of our favorite writers. We were both fans of Thomas Bernhard, I remember,

and it occurred to me that the client's austere way of living—alone, with a few books and some necessary things,
all of a rare, expensive quality—was similar to how I
believe the mature Bernhard lived in Austria.

Outside, climbing into yet another taxi to go back
downtown, my pockets full of money, I felt as if my life
were improving.

On a Saturday night I was to work in a midpriced
Times Square hotel. The agent said he'd only agreed to
send someone to this inferior address because the client
was an out-of-town regular; and he was only staying in
this pedestrian hotel because there were no vacancies at
his usual, fancier hotel. I was greeted by a diffident, fat
man with glasses—a computer programmer from Wash-
ington, D.C. The air conditioner hummed in the chilly
room while we quietly removed our clothing and lay
down on the bed. The man said that he wanted to be
touched very, very gently; and in fact he wanted to be
touched almost not at all, for about half an hour. I slowly
stroked various parts of his body with the extreme tips
of my fingers, occasionally pausing to rest my arm,
which I held in the cool air above the large man's skin
while my fingers did their delicate work below. The
client's body was round and pale and almost completely

hairless. He lay with his eyes closed, taking short, shallow breaths through his mouth, and at what seemed to me an arbitrary moment in our exquisitely calm session, he sighed softly and released the subtle sexual tension he'd been holding inside himself.

Immediately afterward, he got up and washed in the bathroom, and then dressed. I followed suit, and left with the money I had earned with such remarkable ease. I had enjoyed our session, and I envied that man his sensitivity and the refinement of his sexuality, which I suspect gives him uncommon pleasure when he chooses to indulge it.

I worked for a number of famous men. One of them I grew up watching on television, where his persona was that of a freak. I've heard that he is still a regular object of scorn on David Letterman's show. He was normal enough in bed, though. He offered me a plastic bottle of water when I arrived, and led me through several darkened rooms to the back of his large hotel suite, which he said he rented year-round even though he spent most of his time in California. He answered the telephone once during the hour, telling someone that he was just relaxing and was going for a run in Central Park later. He spoke to the person affectionately and

softly, almost as if he were addressing a child, though I
don't believe he was. I massaged the man's body and he
sucked my dick, but mostly he just wanted to kiss me
and hold me, which I found uncomfortable and strange.
He was trying to comfort me, it seemed, and I didn't
know what for. I have always appreciated being com-
forted, and I can usually think of something that puts
me in need of it—some pain or some memory of pain.
But I was distracted by the television image I had of this
man from my childhood, and it seemed absurd that he
should be directing this intimate attention toward me.

He told me afterward about a book he was writing,
which sounded something shy of promising. He under-
paid me by ten dollars, which I didn't notice until I had
left the hotel, and he said goodnight to me in the same
careful, condescending tone he had used with the person on the phone. I found him completely unlikeable.

I was nearly sent to a famous fashion designer, but my
agent decided against it because he said the "blizzard" of
cocaine had lately made things at the man's townhouse
uncontrollable. Several escorts, he said, had left without
collecting any money for fear of not getting safely away.

❧

After my first night of working for the agency with John in the Carlyle, I started doing several jobs a week, and then more. I learned to relax and perform better. With some clients I could enjoy myself, and I reached orgasm myself many times, usually by fantasizing about someone other than the client. I was never tempted not to take my pay, nor did a client ever suggest it.

I liked the freedom of the job, since I was never required to work, only requested; and apart from its disruption of my life, I liked the startling feeling of my pager vibrating against my thigh, telling me that I would be in bed with a new man within the hour, making money.

The one thing that all of my experiences with this first agency had in common was that the time I spent with these men was quiet and unhurried. It was often, for me, similar to meditation of a kind: we were both focused, breathing, and relatively undistracted. We were together in a structured, mysterious way for about an hour. And then, a little richer, I would go away.

28 June 96

Out in the sun. Just finished Portrait of the Artist *again. That last line: "Old father, old artificer, stand me now and ever in good stead." Well, doesn't that just about sum things up, that last line? What an amazing intellectual instinct, to go from father to artificer to salvation in one brand new sentence at the end of a book whose meaning was invented by the author only then, at the end of it. I'll never believe that Joyce had that sentence in mind before the moment of writing it as the last line of his first great book. Saw Tom last night, who was flirting and saying crazy things, high. He thinks he can just breezily have everything he wants. He was telling me about how good the sex with his new boyfriend is. I was there with a guy I was embarrassed by, and left early.*

19 July 96

Long night. Dinner with D. and Toby—she with her cane, he with his aluminum walker. She could hear almost nothing— her hearing is getting much worse. But I played the Bach 3rd English suite "badly, but with feeling," especially the sarabande, and she seemed able to hear that. Toby was, as always, adorable all night. Why do I need to spend so much time with old people? Well, I do need it. It calms me, and these people fascinate me, and I love them. After we put D. to bed and I put

Toby into a cab, I met Richard at Barracuda and we picked up a Cuban model, did some coke, and went to the East Village, where I made out with the model on a sofa while Richard—who was not invited to join us, as he should have been—chatted with strangers. Eventually the model left and I went back to Richard with a word or two about feeling guilty. I wish R. wasn't so blithely accepting of my abuse. I need a fight.

1 September 96, London
The end of a wild weekend. Our little seaside holiday was fun, four of us in a tiny trailer, going to the beach, and of course a good deal of drinking and eating, not to mention finishing off the last gram of coke. Just back from "Gay Night" at Boom Boom, Betsy's neighborhood bar. There were seven people there, plus Paul the barman who says he's straight. Says he wants to move to NYC and took my number. He was wearing the most outrageous headband that said "To be this handsome constitutes the nobility." He's become the household joke here at Betsy's. But he is damned good looking.

8 September 96, Heathrow
Headed home after what feels like quite a long time away—but only about two weeks. The last few days with Betsy have been bizarre. On Friday we started drinking at noon and by 4:00 we'd

bought some coke and spent the evening snorting it and listening to the Sex Pistols. I nearly got a tattoo, but we couldn't decide on a design.

11 September 96

An intense re-entry to NYC. Last night I went to an interview with Wow Agency, an escort service. Later that night they gave me my first job, a "date" with John, an old Texas businessman, married, ex-diplomat, etc. We had drinks in the Carlyle Hotel bar (where he was staying) and then worked at having sex for about an hour. I achieved about half a hard-on late in the proceedings, but he didn't seem too bent on wild sex anyway. I made $240 for two hours' work. Betsy, who just phoned, was impressed. No time to write anything. The cats have fleas, which are everywhere, and one of the cats seems to be missing again. Chaos as usual.

14 September 96

The adventures continue. Worked again last night, for Jim, a lawyer who supposedly hires a hustler every night. It was pretty easy money, $160 for an hour that included having a drink and watching some baseball on TV, giving him a quick massage, getting fucked for a few seconds and then helping him to get off. Prior to that, dinner with D., who was wonderful as always.

Then I saw Richard at Q and got very high. Walked over to the Boiler Room and saw Jay, who sees Tom all the time. He said they spoke of me yesterday, saying they both "really like" me. Big deal. Finally I took a cab toward Toby's, where I'm staying while he's away, but went to the piers where I met Michael, a very strange and sexy guy. Fucked him. Sweet. I borrowed a videotape from him that's marked "Kinky Porn." Haven't seen it yet.

16 September 96

Feeling very strange after watching a horrible porn film I borrowed from Michael, the weirdo I picked up the other night on the piers. It's like I've seen evil for the first time. The tape was actually a snuff film that showed hooded men torturing and surely eventually killing, naked women. It was really one of the most gruesome things I can imagine seeing, and I'm very sorry that I saw it. I can hardly believe it exists. It's been a long time since I was so upset by anything. But of course I was not forced to watch it: I sat there alone, wide-eyed and shocked, and let the tape run on and on without shedding a tear.

17 September 96

Very strange time in my head. The novel's been rejected again. I've been hustling nearly every night for Wow. Yesterday was

Juan from Peru, who desperately wanted me to fuck him, but I couldn't get quite hard. This hustling seriously affects my life, I know. Last night I picked up Craig, a very cute boy, at the Boiler Room. Brought him back here, had no desire for sex with him, and he finally left. I, coked up to my ears, was left to sleeplessness and sexless masturbation. I dreamed I had fleas on my legs and that I was arrested by three police officers in terrible fake fur outfits. I'm asking myself if I can live with being a failure, and coming up with no straight answer. Last night I wouldn't have minded taking a handful of pills if I'd been sure I would never have woken up again—except, except, I guess just sitting here writing this, and going out and snorting cocaine and coming home, is better than being dead—except I just find it very hard to live with myself, having disappointed myself— which I'm not even a hundred percent certain I have done. I think my novel is good, actually, and I think I'm a pretty decent person—but I am isolated, increasingly so. Ehh, this is all so much confusion and bullshit.

21 September 96

Just back from a hustling job, neither easy nor hard, just typical. Another lonely middle-aged man in a dreary apartment. Today I saw My Fair Lady, *the movie, with Don. Gorgeous costumes and sets by Cecil Beaton. Last night Charles and I went to the Philharmonic. Tchaikovsky's Fourth was great, and Vladimir Feltsman played amazing Schnittke cadenzas in the Mozart c minor concerto.*

23 September 96

Met Charles and Brian for drinks and they left with each other. I picked up Jason, a bartender, brought him home and fucked him. A little banal, but I suppose it fills some weird need in me to have sex with a stranger of my choice.

6 October 96

Went with Jonathan and Jenifer and Jane to Belmont Park for horse races. We bet against the world-famous Cigar and won—I won two races and paid for the day. I adore Jane, who's tiny and beautiful. And Jonathan and Jenifer are great friends of mine.

7 October 96

I wish I could do what I want to do: stay at home and work rather than go out and find trouble at any cost. But I know I will go out soon. Reading Virginia Woolf's diaries. How effortlessly the excellent writing seems to pour out of her. As if the world collaborated with her and helped her along, rather than presenting her with dead ends and solid objects that resist meaning. What was her secret? Surely it was not just the good luck of having been at the right place at the right time with the right people. But I often feel that I am obstructed in just this way: the wrong place, the wrong time, the wrong people.

10 October 96

Drug days again. Last night I ran into John, who had coke and was with friends, so we went out and got more coke and went to Jay's, which was weird but fun. Brought John home and fucked him silly. Up til 8:00.

2.

My dictionary defines prostitution as "the act or practice of indulging in promiscuous sexual relations esp. for money" and "the state of being prostituted: DEBASEMENT." As an ex-prostitute, I find this definition a little troubling; I had thought it would emphasize money rather than *debasement*, a word I find outdated almost to the point of meaninglessness. Getting debased is what young women do in Thomas Hardy novels. And Antonio Porchia says, "He who remains with himself a great deal becomes debased." But though I have sometimes felt anxiety about being (and feeling) apart from other people, I have not often been reclusive; though I have isolated myself sometimes, I was never alone for long. Nowadays, I suppose, one could say that politics is debased, but that is rather a different use of the word. And what does "the state of being prostituted" feel like? I simply had sex with people in exchange for money. It's not that I don't concern myself with my social status and the quality of my character; I do. But hustling, at least at the time I began doing it full-time, seemed more like an effective way to earn money than a spiritual or moral dilemma. I do not believe prostitution is particularly objectionable or necessarily depressing for everyone. But the truth is, there is more to hustling than sex, and writing this book is my attempt to come to terms with what is a more insidious habit and a more complicated psychological situation than I originally believed.

It has been a few months, as I write this, since I last hustled. One of my regular clients, Bill, has been calling me again lately, and I have only been putting him off with excuses, unwilling so far to cut the connection completely with such a generous and friendly customer; but I will probably not see him again. I have decided to stop hustling. I find it difficult to imagine myself now—after only a few months—in bed with someone I find sexually unattractive. It seems, contrary to my experience working on and off for about two years as a prostitute, not worth the money. Bill, who is a very intelligent lawyer with whom I share interests in music and books, gave me $350 for about two hours of my time. (We agreed to stop paying the agency long ago, so all the money was mine.) Of that time, only a small fraction of it was spent in his bed, and the sex was relaxed (for me), brief, unimpressive. It was easy money, and I was with Bill many times. Suddenly, however, I don't wish to be with him again. But I do return his calls, and I invent reasons for not being able to see him just now. I could certainly use the money, which will probably always be the case.

Bill often asked me why I was with him. Normally such a question would be considered—especially by someone as self-conscious and well mannered as Bill— to be in poor taste, since it is understood that what I say in response will be a lie. Bill knew why I consented to have sex with him. But he always asked the question when we were in bed, when my persona was predictably unrational and soothing. I would say, Because I like you. Or, Because it's fun, coming over here. I always lied, and for me this mendacity was the most exhausting aspect of the job. I was always pretending to be somebody's friend when I really only wanted his money. Of course this is just an extreme form of something we all do in order to get ahead, but such seeming friendliness is never good or heartfelt and it is always a cause, at least for me, of mental and emotional fatigue.

What I did with Bill, for his money, was humiliating. That seems obvious to me now, but I defended myself against this humiliation for a long time by not admitting it to anyone and not thinking about it. I suspect that Bill would have a hard time understanding this at all—he surely did not mean to humiliate me. I believe, in fact, that

Bill's intentions were probably decent. He wanted to help me with money, and he always treated me with concern and tenderness. But Bill's kindness might have been a good defense for him against the knowledge that I was behaving self-destructively. Even his solicitude was, in its way, humiliating for me, since it came with the understanding that I needed it. Bill and I together fostered a relationship that seriously damaged my self-respect, and we were dishonest about it. The same is true, to some extent, of the relationships I had with all the clients I worked for, most of which lasted for only about an hour.

I lived, for a while, as if repressing certain things was not only acceptable but somehow deeply appropriate. I had a mounting feeling that my life had become sufficiently corrupt that there was a kind of justice in my decision to disregard my feelings and my thoughts. I had done *enough* thinking, *enough* feeling, *enough* believing in the myths of progress and self-development and emotional work. The bets I had placed on myself—as a writer, as an intellectual, as a loving and lovable human being—were not paying off. It may have been vainglorious to have expected satisfaction in my twenties, but I was genuinely disheartened at the time. I was drawn to the night because it seemed more compatible with my real self than daytime had turned out to be. I'd been spurned by a man I loved, my first novel was unpublished, and I was not ambitious in terms of a money-making job. I didn't *want* a job. Perhaps what I really wanted was to settle the score with my father, who does not speak to me. I haven't seen him in twelve years, and he hasn't answered any of my letters. But I love him because he is my dad, and it is probably my love for him more than my hate that drives me to seek some kind of poetic justice—or any kind of justice. I like the idea that my behavior might represent some kind of revenge against my father, even if he never finds out about it. I used to fantasize about ringing my father's doorbell and beating him senseless. But taking money from men who reminded me of my dad in exchange for sex, which I associate with him, hurts him more, in my mind, than anything violent ever could. If my dad can't bear the fact that I'm gay, then how could he feel about being the man for whom all of my customers served as a symbol? This imaginary pain gives me little pleasure, but I don't need pleasure: I need something to compensate for not feeling loved by my father.

On the other hand, I'm sure that what I crave even more than revenge against my father is to be closer to him. Hustling allowed me to act out intimacy with men roughly my father's age, and getting paid for it gave me the resolve to do it, which I normally lack. Older men frighten me sexually; but the money they gave me compensated for the fear, and it seemed at the time like a bargain. I got paid for doing something I was somehow inclined to do anyway, and I felt capable of toughening myself against whatever bad feelings the situations might bring on. I, like prostitutes and gamblers and lovers everywhere, enjoyed for a while the illusion of fearlessness.

But hustling quickly became just another of my bad habits—along with drinking, smoking, taking drugs, shoplifting, lying, and having sex with strangers. I don't know for sure what hustling meant for me, but there was something about it that I liked, beginning perhaps with its sheer perversity. I like sex, and I feel that I understand what many men long for, and I usually knew how to give them what they wanted. Maybe not so well as certain other people know how, but well enough all the same. I was good at it. A good hustler knows that sex is important, but that contact with another human body is even more important—it's something all people need at some times in their lives, for whatever reasons—and it's hard to get enough of it.

I would not be at all ashamed of paying for good sex, and for those of my clients who were looking for that I felt no embarrassment. Good sex is worth paying for if you have the money, just as a good concert is worth the price of admission, or a good meal is justifiably expensive. I admired some of my clients: some of them had worked hard for their money, kept themselves in good shape, and liked to have a good time. Some of them were also affectionate in a way that I liked. And some of them had an aura of serious money and considerable power, and they smelled good, and they did whatever they wanted to do, and I liked that type of man, too: rich, intelligent, worldly, fit. When that kind of man eagerly paid me to spend an hour with him at home, I got more from it than just the money.

Bill was not a paternal type. He tried, I believe, to think of us as equals, even as lovers, rather than as a poor young man hustling a rich older one. He didn't want to think honestly about why I was with him, and he didn't want to be my father. What he really wanted was good sex with a lover, which he had never had. So we pretended to be lovers, and we tried to have good sex together. And sometimes the sex was, in its way, pretty good.

All of my sessions with Bill followed the same pattern.

I would say hello to the doorman and wonder what he thought I was doing there and go up in the elevator to the fourth floor. Bill's dog would be barking hello from behind the door, and just to make the two of them a little crazy, I would give the bell a good long ring. Bill would open up the door in his fancy English robe and kiss me while the dog jumped around madly and barked. I liked the dog, and would always play with him while Bill fixed me a strong drink. The dog and I would go to the sitting room and Bill would come in and smile at us and give me my drink and tell the dog to go lie down. Bill was always in the middle of a stitch in his needlepoint project—a royal crown pillow cover—which he never finished in the year or so that I knew him. The television would be on, and we would watch it for about forty-five seconds while Bill finished his stitch, and then he would push the big wooden stretcher away and press a button on the remote control to turn off the TV. We were ready for our gentlemanly conversation. We talked about opera and books, mostly, and the various projects with which we were involved at the time—Bill was organizing a large event for an Ivy League club he belonged to, and I was always looking for a job and writing something. These conversations were occasionally awkward because I wasn't always in the mood for them and was often very high and a little drunk; but usually I enjoyed talking with Bill about the aspects of our lives that were pleasant or promising.

After about an hour I would get up to use the bathroom and tell Bill that I would meet him in the other room. In the bathroom I usually snorted some speed and then washed my face and hands with Bill's expensive honey-scented soap. When I got to Bill's bedroom, he was on his bed wearing boxer shorts. I would leisurely take off my clothes (except my underwear, which Bill liked to remove himself) while looking around at the books Bill was reading, and I'd ask him if they were any good, and he would tell me about them—mostly Englishy mysteries and historical novels about aristocrats and murderers.

Finally I would jump up on Bill's big four-poster canopied bed in my briefs and give him a playful kiss. Kissing an overweight man in his sixties takes some getting used to, but even a fat, older man is nothing more or less than a man, and if your true aim at that moment is to please him, kissing him can become a kind of mysterious pleasure. My *true* aim, of course, was to get paid and to be on my way; but there is room for a kind of virtual sincerity within that context. The sexual pleasure of kissing

someone like Bill was not real for me at first. But I discovered that if I made it *look* real enough, and if I did it
for long enough a time, it could become a real pleasure—in the same way that a person's façade, in time, can
become his soul. After the first few sessions with Bill, I
began to enjoy kissing him, and I even enjoyed the feel
of his body. He was hairless and large, but not flabby or
too soft, and he had no odor or bad breath. His penis
was not large, and it sometimes took some time before it
became erect—usually he would get hard after he had
been touching my ass. Most of my clients were eager to
suck my dick, but not Bill. He liked to look at and caress
my ass, and he would talk about fucking me, and I
would encourage him—though he never tried actually
to do it, and I certainly never suggested it. While Bill
explored my butt, I sucked his dick, which is something
I did only for good, regular clients.

I was aroused by Bill's apparently intense pleasure and
by the crystal meth I had snorted in the bathroom. I
usually got a hard-on, and I often came after Bill did. I
always brought Bill to his orgasm in the same way. After
sucking his dick for a few minutes, I would sense by his
breathing, which became very heavy and fast, that he
was ready. With Bill lying on his back, I would sit up on

my knees with my ass above his left hand and I'd hold his cock very lightly and stroke it, with the slightest pressure, near the head, and Bill would squirm and moan. He would put the tip of a finger into my ass, which he had been waiting a long time to do, and this combination of thrills would instantly produce for him a rather slow, long orgasm that made Bill shudder and throb and moan and breathe. Then, when I felt like it, I would turn around and close my eyes and imagine a sexy situation with someone else and manage to come on Bill's chest, and then collapse on top of him. We would hold each other for a few minutes before I excused myself, leaving him still and spent on his bed.

When I emerged from his bathroom a few minutes later, Bill was always smiling. He always said something about how beautiful I was and how much he had enjoyed himself, and I would grin and put my clothes on. Bill would shuffle out to the study in his robe and slippers, write me a check, and send me home with a kiss goodnight.

૯৩

Working as an escort is not easy, physically or otherwise, and it can serve as a good justification for a lot of questionable behavior such as taking drugs, sleeping around, going out too much at night, and not having a better job. If artistic ambitions are involved, as in my case, since I thought of myself as a writer, the justification is all the more appealing because escorts make their money fast and thus ostensibly have more free time than most people do. I have spent months at a time working only an hour a day, and there was a brief time when I had two regular clients (including Bill) whose combined fee was all the money I needed; seeing both of them took up less than four hours of my week. But regular clients were rarely regular for long; one reason prostitution is called hustling is that work is not always steady. Among the pleasures of hiring an escort is surely the anticipation of meeting a ravishing stranger. After a while Bill just stopped calling, and I didn't hear from him for six months. He had told me that he liked talking to me and he said he admired my writing—he'd read some book reviews of mine in a newspaper. The other client had said he liked my body. But these passions apparently faded, and I was left to find new clients once again. I used to think about Bill, with whom I had those long conversations, and I was sorry our arrangement ended when it did. Despite the fact that I saw him for his money, I liked him, and I felt that he liked me. He deplored drugs and excess of any kind—he fancied himself a real gentleman, and I tended to tell him the truth about the things going on in my life. I told him all sorts of terrible things about my nocturnal adventures, knowing that he would be censorious, and his disapproval felt to me at times almost like a form of love. And as it happened I could have used such a form of love around the time Bill stopped calling me—which was toward the nearly disastrous end of my time as a full-time prostitute.

Early in the fall of 1997 (which is when I met Bill), I got back to New York after having spent the summer in the Southwest working for a performing arts festival. The summer had not been a good one: I did not like my job, did not make many friends, and gambled away most of the money I earned at work learning to play poker at a casino, which I loved (and which became another addiction I'm still struggling to relinquish). I found the job in February when a good friend said I should get one, implying that I was strung out and pathetic. He was right, and I knew it. The job began in New York almost immediately, and I was told that I would be going away for the summer. I welcomed the opportunity to clean up my life, because in addition to hustling every night, I had been taking some serious drugs, including heroin. I had not been writing anything, and my life was a mess.

I used credit cards to buy some suits and worried about how I would manage to wake up on time for my first day of work. But I did get up, and things improved— or anyway I got clean for a while from drugs and hustling. My job was dull, my boss was a monster, and I felt ridiculous on the bus, in a suit, at 8:30 in the morning. I couldn't help feeling that I *belonged* again to the class of people who get up for work in the morning, who live within the constraints of the law, who go to bed at night and have good or bad or indifferent sex on a regular, reasonable schedule. And I didn't want to belong—I never really have. It seemed crazy to be earning less in a whole day than I had earned a week before in one hour, and to allow myself to be humiliated in other and possibly more damaging ways. I hated my boss and his small, superior virtue. I hated the association with ordinary ambition, with office chatter and breakfast meetings and saving up money for retirement. But I did it, determined to change.

I went to New Mexico and passed the summer there. I had a couple of unimportant romances, went hiking with a friend and a guy from Albuquerque, gambled a lot, drove around the desert looking in vain for peace of mind, enjoyed the scenery and the lightning storms and the wide open spaces and the clear, dry, thin desert air.

I could hardly wait to get back to New York, and when my boss told me at the end of the summer that I could leave—and not come back—I drove home, twenty-four hundred miles in three days of rain, sleet, sun, and rock 'n' roll on the radio. I'd found some coke before I left, and I made it last until halfway through New Jersey, which was just long enough.

I got to New York at 3 A.M. on a Thursday morning and went straight to the sauna. I was in desperate need of chemical stimulation by then, and I was looking for more cocaine when somebody offered to sell me some crystal methamphetamine, "the Dom Perignon of speed." I bought some that night, then I bought the stuff on a regular basis and snorted it every day and night for the next four months. I was addicted within about a week, though I did not consider my use an addiction at the time. To pay for my new drug (which is not cheap), and to live the way I wanted to live at the time, and for some reason which to this day I cannot quite put my finger on but which has something to do with being addicted

to sexual shame, I started hustling again, this time with a
vengeance, or a passion.

My desert cure—my clean summer—was over. And I
was glad.

13 October 96

Went with C. to Monte Carlo Ballet last night, then to dinner and the Boiler Room, then home where I came down from coke and was a little drunk and went into a very deep depression. Poor C. talked me through it, and was very patient and sweet, and then he fucked me, all of which helped. He's right, though, that I must lay off the coke, because it just emphasizes my manic-depressive personality and last night the depressive part was feeling pretty nearly unendurable—though of course it wasn't actually, at least not with C. there with me. And here in NYC it is almost never necessary to be absolutely alone. But that's no justification for facilitating an awful funk.

16 October 96

Saw Toby, who's recovering from his hip operation. I clipped his toenails for him, which we agreed was a pretty intimate little business. Last night John said my hustling makes him jealous, and that if we're to date each other, I'd better stop it. I told him I would. Actually, I haven't had any work from them in some time now, so it doesn't require much willpower to stop. If they call tonight, while John is away, I'll probably do the job, jerk that I am—or poor as I am, or fucked up, or whatever I am. I am feeling very distinctly fucked up lately. I saw Brett the other night and told him about my problems. He wisely said I was changing—and changing hurts. I'm sure he's right. Anyway there are far worse things than disliking the idea of staying home alone, and fighting the urge to go out—and getting depressed after doing cocaine. Real suffering will no doubt present itself to me in due course.

19 October 96

Worked last night for Wow. A very dumb banker from Seattle. When he asked what I was reading (I had a paperback in my pocket) and I said Freud, he said, What's that, a novel? The hour passed—a massage and then some odd activity involving the guy's little penis. Before working I saw Toby, who is not very well. I took him a pizza, which he loved.

20 October 96

Fasted all day as an experiment in "spiritual hygiene." Gave me a headache and a dull depression. I don't feel particularly cleansed, either.

26 October 96

Great dinner with D. last night. I played a Haydn sonata for her, and the aria from the Goldberg Variations. When I finished, I looked over and she was sitting with her eyes closed, and after a while she said that it had been very moving. Later

*that night, coming home from La Bonne Soupe, she said I was
a great strength for her. I feel as if we're falling in love with each
other—or as if our love is deepening—on a macabre schedule
corresponding, almost operatically, with her oncoming death
(she's ninety-six now!). I must be prepared for a painful sepa-
ration—the one thing I really am not prepared for right now.
Very dreary night at the sauna afterward.*

10 November 96

*Trying, not very successfully, to get onto a more ordinary sched-
ule. Woke up again today at 12:30 P.M. Couldn't sleep until
about 4:30. Reading* Brighton Rock. *Went early to the sauna,
fucked a cute Brazilian, and came home. Tonight is a dinner for
Charles's birthday.*

15 November 96

Reading Kierkegaard's Fear and Trembling. *"Faith" has sort
of presented itself to me lately in an unusual way. I never gave
it all that much thought before. But I must say that K.'s awe for
the "Knight of Faith" affects me deeply. I love his description of
the process: first, resignation (out of a kind of depression, I
would say)—a gesture toward the infinite. This, along with K.,
I can understand. The position of the tragic hero—the focus on
an object of passion that requires sacrifice, leading to a real or*

imagined suicide. Like the troubadours. But it's the next step that's intriguing to me now, and mystical: toward finitude. A gesture toward the absurd, saying, in effect: I will make this sacrifice—of this thing that I love above myself and above all else—and I know, by some absurd faith, that I will recover it somehow, sometime, and gain grace for having suffered the loss.

16 November 96

Found a poem by Frederick Seidel in an anthology. It ends: "Convinced life is meaningless/ I lack the courage of my conviction."

18 November 96

Very wild weekend. Lots of work and drugs. I may not be getting much writing done, and I may have a lot of bad habits, but I am having one hell of a time (and making a lot of money).

3.

I was raised in the thick of sex, or so I tend to believe. The proximity—the noise, and the insistence—of adult sex in the houses I grew up in gave sex an aura of profound, attractive mystery that still holds a great sway over me. I longed as a child for a powerful sexual experience of my own, and I still do as an adult (despite having had some). When I was young I already craved sexual attention, even if from someone much older than I—my imagination led me to believe that I could be excited and perhaps satisfied by almost any sort of sexual encounter. I recall having a secret crush on a man who was known to be gay when I was about thirteen, though I did not have the courage to flirt with him. He and his lover must have been in their fifties. It was, no doubt, a good thing that I was not able to act on that particular desire—whatever might have happened would probably have been disturbing. I did have sex with boys and girls my own age beginning when I was about eight.

I was aware from an early age that my parents had an inscrutable habit of doing things with each other in their bedroom at night other than just talking and sleeping. They sometimes giggled, and they often fought, and they made entirely too much noise. I resented it because I didn't know what to make of it, and they were never inclined to talk about it the next day (though I never asked). I assumed they were fighting and making up— but about what? I knew their behavior was somehow erotic, and I wanted to see, or at least to know, in just what way it was erotic. I had the feeling that my mother was surrendering to my dad on these nights; my father was always drunk, and mean when he was drunk, so what else could she have been doing when she consented to giggle?

My earliest memories of my father (and most of my later ones) are all colored by aggression and sex. I remember him coming home one night, drunk, and stumbling into my night-lighted bedroom to apologize for something: the only time I remember him kissing me (or apologizing to me), he drooled and slobbered. He tasted and smelled like a bad man, and though I certainly wanted his love, I did not want it just then. I don't really know exactly what happened that night, or why my father was there in my room, but his horrid kisses were confusing for me, and I have come to believe that few things are worse for a small child than being teased and confused with a parent's love. He gave me the feeling then and often afterward that his love could be available to his son, but not to me. Symbols for my father's love, in all its dazzling ambiguity, are surely at least part of what I seek from all the men with whom I come into close contact.

I grew up in small towns near Dayton, Ohio. My father worked as a signalman for a railroad company, and my mother worked in factories, first making ice buckets and later as a welder in a bicycle factory. My father was my mother's second husband, and my older sister had the earlier husband, whom I never met, as her father. He died in a motorcycle crash when I was about twelve. My father was in the Air Force, and he was stationed in Korea when I was born. My mother told me a few years ago that he suspected I was not his child, but she assures me that I am. I believe she told me about his suspicion in order to explain his prejudice against me now and his abuse of me when I was young. I find it just as easy to believe that he resents the fact that I'm gay and that when I was a child, he was abusive of his whole family because he was a violent, alcoholic, confused, and unhappy man.

My father was a fanatical softball player, a fan of baseball teams and beer. He was the softball home run champion in the state of Ohio one year, and he made some extra money playing professionally. Hired to do little more than hit the ball as often as the team could put him up to bat, I gather that he almost always hit home runs. His bedroom was cluttered with trophies. Another kind of son would have been proud, but I was only dimly aware of his prowess and did not connect with it emotionally, which I regret. My father was never my friend; he was always an intimidating, dangerous stranger whose arrival at home after work filled me with dread. I remember going with him to the ballpark. I can hear the sound of his cleats on the gravel in the parking lot. I can see those terrible bright lights around the field, and all those bugs and families. I remember the candy we kids ate, a kind of sweet, sour sugar in a long straw, and the horsing around we did under the bleachers, which was great fun, and falling asleep in the back seat of the car on the way home. But I don't remember seeing my dad play ball, or hit any of those home runs he was locally so famous for. I didn't care about it. Softball and I were just not meant for each other, and I suppose the same must be said for my dad and me.

A handful of children are blessed with parents who provide them with an appropriate amount of good information about sex; many children are told nothing; and some see too much and are told the wrong things. I fell into this last category. After my parents divorced, when I was eight, my mother enjoyed a sexual liberation and her three children were compelled to enjoy it, too— or to witness it, anyway. My mother, my sister, my younger brother, and I moved into a two-bedroom mobile home in a trailer park. (The trailer was far from paid for and totally uninsured when it and everything in it burned about a year later, one week before Christmas. I remember watching it burn, late at night, from a neighbor's trailer across the street, and being amazed at the brightness of it: the whole thing was in roaring, wicked flames.) My mother had a succession of boyfriends, and she apparently felt free to indulge her sexuality without worrying too much about the effects it might have on her three children. I have an especially vivid memory of a noisy man in the trailer making a joke about condoms, which I only slowly and partially understood, but I knew right away that it was nasty, and I felt both titillated and wounded by it. My siblings and I were able to hear the erotic noises that issued nearly every night (or so it seemed), and sometimes during the day, from our mother's bedroom down the short, narrow hallway. Her appetite for sex was evidently powerful, and I believe, to simplify the psychology, that I inherited it.

One of my mom's boyfriends had a white Corvette, and for some reason I was once taken along in it to the home of some adult friends of the boyfriend. The house was near a lake, and it was a long day of fishing and swimming, and then everyone went into the house for dinner. After dinner, we all settled down around the television and watched a porn film—my first. I was about twelve. I remember my mother expressing some doubt about the appropriateness of the experience for me, but her boyfriend assured her that it was okay.

Eventually my mother remarried and became pregnant again. We relocated to the town where she had grown up and where her parents and her new husband lived, and we moved in with him. He was a drug addict and a newly converted Christian (at the same time) and he took the Bible (or parts of it) very seriously. One Christmas Eve, we kids wanted to watch a special cartoon on television; he wanted to read aloud from the Bible instead. Ultimately he gave up and furiously threw his big Bible across the room, frightening all of us and spoiling the evening. I never liked him and never knew what my mother might have seen in him. They divorced during my mother's pregnancy with my younger sister. Years later when I was home from college for a weekend, he and I had a fistfight at his house. My sister (his daughter) was scheduled to spend time with him that weekend, but she wanted to come home early to see me. He refused to bring her home, so my mother and I went to get her. When we arrived, he was in a rage and when he went aggressively toward my mother, I intervened. We fought to the point of bloody noses and black eyes. My mother and little sister got into the car, but they couldn't drive away. The car keys were in my pocket. While I ran to a neighbor's to phone the police, my mother and adorable eight-year-old sister cowered in the car as George beat on the windshield with a branch from a tree, yelling at them to come out, or to let him in. That was the last time my sister ever saw her father, who died six months later under mysterious circumstances.

After that husband and more boyfriends, my mother married one of her high school sweethearts who had just been released from prison. He swore to her that he wanted nothing but a quiet family life with us from then on, and my mother must have believed him because she married him two weeks later. I took the day off from school (I was in the eighth grade) to bear witness to the wedding, and a month or two later I had a loaded shotgun to my head: the husband thought I

got in the way of his relationship with my mother. He
hated me and said he would kill me before I came
between the two of them. Eventually we drove away
from our own house in order to escape yet another of
my mother's menacing husbands. He had decided that
if the marriage could not be made to work—on his
violent, ludicrous terms—he would sooner kill us than
leave us. The whole episode with him seems like some
kind of unbelievable melodrama to me now. I had
nightmares about him for years. The last I heard he was
back in prison. I'd be curious to know for what crime.

While I do not remember being consciously opposed
to the idea of my mother being married, I was disappointed whenever, after she left my father, she slept with
someone else. I had developed the habit of sleeping with
her in her bed. I don't remember whose idea it was, and
nothing overtly sexual ever happened, but I loved the
warmth of her body, and the feel of her nightgown, and
the smell of her breath. Sometimes she would lull me to
sleep beside her by grazing the skin of my bare back
with her fingernails, very softly. This went on until I was
about fourteen. When she had a boyfriend or a husband,
it was understood, I slept alone.

My mother married yet another man I didn't like

while I was still living at home. He was a construction worker a little more than half my mother's age. His first name was Mark, but I've just realized that I don't even remember his last name, which was my mother's name for a while. He was another drinker, but my main complaint with this one was that he was boring; he was also overweight, slept with other women, spent most of his money on himself and his own two small children, and he swore too much. Before they were married, when I was a teenager, Mark and my mom fucked on the sofa in the living room one night. I was upstairs in bed, but I was able to hear them and became really disturbed by the vivid knowledge (or fantasy) of what he was doing to her, and what she was doing with him. We lived next door to a family I had become very close to, and the father was my best friend. In the dead of winter, I got up from bed wearing nothing but my underwear. In a kind of blank trance (I was normally not a dramatic or flamboyant boy), I went down the stairs, past the open living room door, out onto the snow and across the yard, and banged on my friend's door. He and his wife came down in their pajamas and took me in. He held me shivering in his bathrobe and calmed me for hours before dressing me in his clothes and taking me home.

My mother would sometimes take me along to a bar in a hotel about twenty minutes from where we lived, where she would meet her girlfriends for a drink. There was live music some nights: a middle-aged man with a bad haircut and an electronic keyboard doing familiar songs. I remember my mother introducing me to her friends as her son, and I was proud to be with her. She was a pretty woman, and many of the men flirted with her. She and I both enjoyed the attention they gave her. She was a good flirt: restrained and a little shy, but obviously capable of lots of fun. There was always a moment during the flirtation—a gesture of tightening her lips and being physically uneasy—when she was demure, or ingenuous. I always hoped she would refuse the man after this decisive moment. Sometimes she did.

My mother gave me an appreciation for having fun. I remember when I was about thirteen, Mom wanted to go to the drive-in to see a movie, which we often did during the summer. My mother never lost her enthusiasm for drive-ins, but on this particular night her four kids had temporarily lost theirs. As dusk came on and the time to leave for the movie approached, my mom tired of prodding us. I vividly recall her standing at the top of the stairs in jeans and a sexy, sleeveless top, saying,

Well, I'm going to have me some fun. Bye, kids. The four of us came running behind her and piled into the car and we all went happily off to the movies.

When I was fifteen I went with one of my mom's boyfriends to California in his eighteen-wheel truck. He was to deliver a shipment of cauliflower to Los Angeles from Ohio in three days, and he hired me to come along to keep him awake. He told me he'd give me a hundred dollars if we didn't crash the truck and die and if we got to L.A. before the cauliflower went bad. I was thrilled. I liked Bill and I liked his big blue truck, and Los Angeles was a place I never imagined I would see. We set off and drove southwesterly all the way down through the panhandle of Texas and toward the deserts. We stopped at truck stops and at every fourth or fifth rest stop along the highway. At a truck stop in Missouri one night we picked up a prostitute because it was raining and she looked cold and miserable. We said she could sit with us for a while and have some coffee. I remember that I liked her, and that she had red hair and freckles. I expected her to be much harder than she seemed—I was surprised by her ordinary vulnerability, and I was relieved that I didn't feel sorry for her. I found her quite glamorous and attractive.

Then we drove into the desert and Bill began to get sleepy. He told me that I (who had slept) would have to drive, and he told me how to shift the gears and how to keep the truck within the lines of the road—and how to stop. I'd already learned how to talk on the CB radio, and how to listen to it in order to avoid the highway patrol. I even had my own CB "handle": Big Daddy. So I drove the big blue truck at eighty miles an hour all the way through Arizona, right into the sunset and then into the night while Bill was sound asleep in the bed behind my seat. He snored louder than anyone I'd ever heard.

When we got to L.A. we visited some relatives of his who took us to Paramount Studios, where we saw Dean Martin coming out of a trailer with a drink in his hand at noon.

When Bill and I got back to Ohio, Bill and my mom went straight to the waterbed and I sat in the kitchen, listening to them fuck. I pissed the bed that night, which Bill later said was a common occurrence after a long trip.

Now my mother is married to her sixth husband, a very nice, harmless man who has been in love with her for many years. There seems to be little sexual attraction on her part, and I imagine their sex life is not very vigorous. I find it deeply ironic that such a benign, friendly relationship should interest my mother now that none of her children lives with her. Perhaps the relationship is not actually as benign as it appears to be. Just the other day, in fact, I asked my mother how the two of them were getting along. I can't stand him, she said, but other than that I guess we get along all right.

As a child, I longed for the daily routine of a mother and father going about their conventional, ordinary business, taking pains to make sure the kids were reasonably happy and well fed, sensible about protecting them from things they shouldn't see or hear, and persuading them that they were loved and safe.

Last Thanksgiving, when I was addicted to crystal meth and hustling every night, I was invited to the home of some journalists for dinner. They had both been married before, but they had been together, in love, for a long time, and they had a beautiful ten-year-old daughter, who was also there for dinner. After we finished eating, we'd all moved to the other end of the apartment; the father of the little girl had taken the sofa and had stretched out comfortably with a glass of port. We sat around talking while the little girl went to her computer to play chess. Occasionally she would let us know how the game was going; her father was particularly interested. She had chosen a challenging level of play, and her father was being skeptical about her chances for success. When she announced that she was on the verge of winning, her father quickly put down his glass and leaped up from his very comfortable position on the sofa. He went to his daughter and watched her win, and then he told her how proud of her he was. He could have said the same thing without getting up from the sofa; but he did get up. He wanted to be persuasive about his love for that lucky little girl.

I'm sure my mother loves me, but I was not always sure and I wish I had been.

I have no idea whether or not my father loves me or if he ever thinks about me, which I try not to worry about too much or dwell on for long. I dreamed about him a year ago and the dream seemed to be the background for my whole sexuality—it almost even, in some obscure way, explained it. He had, in the dream, the perfect cock, and the sexual contact I had with him was pure bliss.

❧

I'm reluctant to assert any direct connection between specific events from my childhood and the way I was recently living. Psychology is surely at least as complex and daunting a subject as, say, cosmology or history, and I don't know myself even as well as I should. I know that I am prone to addiction; that I thrive on rebellion; that I need vast quantities of attention, particularly from men who are smarter, younger, handsomer, or richer than I. I know that I have a neurotic instinct for situations in which I am expected to comply with somebody else's wishes. And I have my suspicions about what in my past must have led me to the enjoyment of full-out sexual humiliation. And that is what it finally was. But psychological speculations are never quite satisfactory—they never *really* explain a person's weakness of will.

Most of the time I did not feel as if I was doing something terribly wrong. It made perfectly good sense to me that I, who have always loved and needed lots of sex, should do it for money. I was, after all, an artist; a writer who chose not to have a regular job because my ambitions were aimed elsewhere. And then it made sense to use crystal meth because it made working so much easier and it felt good and I was having fun. Some people scoff at another person's need for fun; not I. I've had jobs. I've known people driven by the desire to be rich or powerful or both. There is nothing inherently better about working hard all week in an office than working for a couple of hours in a stranger's bedroom— except that a regular job disciplines your day and gives a shape to your life. But so what? I shaped my own days, and my discipline (I thought) came from within. I had never had any real discipline at home when I was young, so I was accustomed to pretending that I knew what to do with myself.

It was like a spiral: I was getting weaker all the time. I was living on money from hustling, and I needed drugs to hustle, so I stopped paying bills—I even stopped making bank deposits—and I said to myself, Fuck it. Just for a while, I said, I'll just do this crazy thing and see what happens. And it felt good—even the going down- ward, *especially* the going downward. It was relaxing and easy. I thought I might die, and I didn't really care much. I had a few good friends, and I relied on them to keep me in the world, and I relied on their love—that became, and remains, very important to me. But at the time, their love was important partly because I thought it would be easier to fade away—to kill myself—sup- ported *just enough* by the love of a few people, instead of completely, bleakly alone. I had made a pact with a suicidal friend: we had agreed not to kill ourselves, for the sake of each other. But I thought that a specific written apology and explanation to her would be enough to keep her alive and to let her, eventually, get past her feelings about me. The fact is, it was the thought of certain friends (including the suicidal one) and of my younger sister that prevented me a couple of times from thinking more seriously about cutting my wrists open, which I thought of as the most appealing way to go.

But in early January 1998, I bottomed out. I was addicted to cocaine and anonymous sex, and I couldn't stand to be alone with myself even for a night. I had to be high in order not to be miserable, but I couldn't sleep (or eat) when I was high. I got home one morning after having finished the coke I had. I found myself alone, without any drugs, and I got really scared. I couldn't think of anything to rely on or to be hopeful about, and I couldn't sleep. I phoned a suicide hotline at 4:30 A.M. because I was afraid that the part of me that wanted to die was going to defeat the part that didn't. A sensible, kind man on the phone talked me eventually into going to sleep. I cried with him on the phone that night—something I hadn't done for a long time. As a child I cried when my father spanked me, which he did every day while I lived with him. My crying then came from pain but it was also meant as a sign: that I'd had enough, that he'd hurt me and could stop. Ever since, crying for me has had a complicated meaning. Whenever I cry, I am reminded of crying for my father, imploring him to stop hitting me, knowing—with a specific, weirdly familiar feeling of dread mixed with some kind of awful excitement—that we would repeat the ritual again the next night, and every night thereafter.

I spent the summer of 1998 in a small, prosperous town in the countryside. Everywhere I looked, it seemed, I found glowing young fathers and their happy, charming sons. I was never sure if I was perceiving these men and their boys the way I did because of something within myself, or if there really were more young fathers around there who happily took their charming little boys out for a good time than there had been in the places where I lived in the past. What amazed me even more was that here in this town, which happens to be famous for its devotion to sports, the fathers seemed careful *not* to bring up their boys as the brutal athletes I have always thought most fathers wanted their sons to become. Almost every day the whole season, I witnessed at least one man in his thirties teaching his son to be thoughtful and polite and civilized. At the gym one day, I was alone in the steam room when a handsome, naked man came in with his two boys, Desi and Curtis, two and six, also nude. The boys loved the heat of the room, and they practically climbed onto my lap, since the seats were too hot. Desi, the younger one, chose after all to stand near his father on a rubber mat on the floor. At one point he reached over and fondled his dad's balls and said, Nice peanuts, and his dad casually, with just a little embarrassment, told him to stop that. They were so comfortable with each other; they loved each other, and they liked being together. Curtis, the older one, stroked his dad's biceps to wipe away some sweat, and I could tell that he admired his dad's strong-looking muscles and he aspired to live, one day, in his father's image. Everything in the world, for these boys, whether it was good or bad, was interesting and exciting—the sauna, the showers afterward, the whole evening—the whole world. It was even fun for them to talk to me, and to tell me where they were from—from down in the valley, about ten miles away.

Landing on my feet, I fled breathlessly down High Street,
through Willow, and was turning into Brierwood Place
when the sound of several voices, calling to me in distress,
stopped my progress.

    —Thomas Bailey Aldrich, *The Story of a Bad Boy*

4.

I came to New York City ten years ago with my
boyfriend, Thaddeus, who happens to have been the
strangest person I've ever known. Between us we had
$1800 in cash (with nothing in the bank) and Thad had
one friend in New York (I had none). We arrived by
Greyhound Bus at Port Authority, each of us carrying
two bags that held everything we owned. We had both
been to New York once before, on separate occasions, and
we were both aspiring artists—Thad was a dancer, and I
thought I wanted to be a musician. We were both twenty
years old, college dropouts, from poor Midwestern families, and we were *on our own*. I was never happier than I
was when that awful bus pulled into Manhattan and
delivered Thad and me to the rest of our lives, for better

or worse. I loved New York passionately, immediately, and permanently.

Three years before going to New York I moved by myself, when I was seventeen, to Cincinnati from a small town two hours north in order to spend my last year of high school at the School for Creative and Performing Arts. I auditioned to get in, and when I was accepted my mother couldn't come up with a good reason for me not to go. There was a single place available in the senior class and it was offered to me. Had I not gone, I believe my life would have turned out very differently, because I was miserable in that small town and something had to change. In Cincinnati, I came alive. I had escaped.

I had a girlfriend in Cincinnati for a while, Annette, an intelligent, sweet girl who reminded me of my older sister. I was flattered by her attention and happy to be attached to a person of either sex, but it wasn't long before I understood that in this city, in this unusual school, I could have a boyfriend if I wanted one, and I responded wholeheartedly to the attention I got from some of the boys in my class. The principal of the school had arranged for me to live with a very kind doctor and his wife who'd been missionaries in Africa. They accepted my new boyfriend, Jim, into "the family" without any hesitation. I left Annette, causing a brief scandal at the school.

There were two single beds in my room, and Jim and I ritually rumpled the second one every night. Mrs. Paine, my temporary mother, would have made both of them neatly up by the time Jim and I got home from school at the end of the day. Jim had breakfast with us every morning, and we were all happy. I had told Dr. and Mrs. Paine that Jim's father was abusive and that Jim couldn't safely spend much time at home, which was true. Whether or not they suspected that Jim and I had sex with each other, I never knew.

Sleeping with my first boyfriend was wonderful. Every night, I discovered some new physical delight, some new way to open myself to Jim, and to give him a new kind of pleasure or succor, another sign of love. Our love was not deep or lasting, but it was love at the time, and it felt good, both giving it and receiving it. We were seventeen years old, and sex with another person was largely unknown to us. Everything that felt good was a sweet revelation, and we didn't feel guilty or unsatisfied or distracted. We were led to what we did with each other by pure instinct, without the influence of pornography or frenzy or boredom. Perhaps I'm idealizing those nights with Jim; if so, I'm nonetheless glad to think of those idealized high school nights in Ohio with that beautiful young guy in my single bed.

During that year, I also met an extraordinary woman named Diane who was an eccentric and brilliant conductor and music teacher. The choir teacher at the high school introduced me to her. She felt that I would benefit from Diane's unusual lessons, which were essentially concerned with deepening the student's capacity for concentration. I found Diane—who was more than twice my age—sexually irresistible, and by the end of the school year I had left Jim and the kind Paines and was living with Diane in her big blue house at the far end of a long, quiet street.

Diane had had a fiery affair with a younger woman that ended not long before we met, and this woman, Ann, would occasionally show up at the house, whereupon Diane would suddenly become suicidal and hysterical. Diane had an Egyptian cat whose tail was longer than its body; the sleek, grey cat's mood depended completely on what was happening in the house, and when Ann came around, the cat would run wildly from room to room so fast that you could barely see it, jumping from the floor to the top of a door and across the kitchen to a butcher block, landing precisely on the small space that was clear of knives and spices. When Ann left, the cat calmed down, and so did Diane. After a visit from Ann, Diane and I would always go out for a long drive in her fabulous black BMW convertible with the top down, and end up someplace far away in Kentucky or Indiana—we always went to *another state*, which was one of Diane's little jokes.

Diane and I had great, athletic sex, though she told me that when she'd had orgasms with Ann they were like "vaginal volcanoes," which put me off for two reasons: because I wasn't likely to produce them for her, and because I found the image disgusting, which Diane and I both took as proof that I (like her) was not heterosexual. She told me many times that I was foolish not to go out and find myself a man. She even tried to set me up with her gay friends; but for a while I was enthralled by Diane and we had a good time together. We had some friends out in the countryside with a huge new house. They were husband and wife, with two daughters; he was confined to a wheelchair, and the house had been built with polished wood ramps and no stairs. One of the balconies faced a lovely field full of sunflowers, and I remember the four of us sitting out there on a stormy afternoon watching the rain and the lightning, and the sunflowers bending down low in the wind. Diane and I had our own bedroom in the house, and we would sit with our friends in the hot tub until two in the morning and then go to bed and fuck until four.

It never occurred to me at the time that I was being "kept," but Diane did pay for everything and we lived in her house and drove her car. She even bought me a motorcycle—a Kawasaki I loved and gave up only after I was arrested for speeding with no insurance, no helmet, no eye protection, and no motorcycle license. If I could be kept again by a woman like Diane, I'd jump at the chance. With her I was totally free to do whatever I wanted, to come and go, to be honest, to listen to Brahms at full volume in the middle of the night, and to be taken care of and held by someone I loved.

But at the end of the summer, I went off to the University of Cincinnati Conservatory of Music to study opera, and lived in a dorm, a few miles from Diane's house. Our friendship, still passionate, became tense and unpredictable. I would have the sudden feeling that Diane was in grave danger, and I would call her house in a panic in the middle of the night. She would be annoyed that I'd woken her up and would tell me to go to sleep and to forget about her. Finally she moved to San Francisco to take a conducting job there. She gave her house and everything in it to Ann in a final hysterical gesture, and then she was gone. She took me for a final drive the day before she left. It was a cold, rainy day and she told me that I probably would not ever see her again. In her car, with the rain pelting down on the canvas roof, she said that it is always best if things are brought to a complete, definite end when they're over. But how do you know it's over? I asked her. Just look at this weather, she said. How could it not be over with weather like this? I was nineteen, and very sad to see her go.

At college, I fell in love for the first time. David was a sculptor who always looked as if he'd been hard at work creating yet another masterpiece. Brooding and intense, David had brilliant friends and a great, ironic sense of humor. I was in love with him before I'd even met him, having seen him on campus and heard intriguing things about him. I made a terrible, unconscious mistake with David, which I would repeat years later with Tom, the other man I have fallen madly in love with: I lost my personality. I became so closely identified with my lover, and worried so much about losing him, that I was really boring and ludicrously sensitive to anything he said

or did that might affect our relationship. In both cases, the
fact that I was in love caused me intense anxiety, and my
insecurity allowed me no opportunity for feeling comfortable in the relationship. I assumed that sooner or later I
would be abandoned; perhaps this unconscious prophecy
was relevant to the fact that it was eventually fulfilled. Still,
I was wildly happy during those fourteen months I spent
sleeping with and talking to and getting to know David,
whom I still miss.

After David left me, during my second year of college, I met Thad, who immediately persuaded me that
the two of us should move to New York. We had, he
implied, exhausted the resources of Cincinnati. We
wanted to be stimulated and driven and challenged. We
wanted to be ourselves, and we were finding it hard to
do that anymore in Cincinnati.

I met Thad at a party where he was sitting off by
himself on the floor, unengaged. He was beautiful, and
looked like a person who was not afraid of getting into
trouble, and this appealed to me. I was nineteen, and life
then was largely a matter of avoiding boredom. I tried
hard, for years, to be fun. Thad and I went off together
that night in search of a good time, and we became
friends, though I never really felt that he liked me par-

ticularly. I sensed that he was troubled and complicated, and I wanted to understand him and help him. I also liked being known as someone with such an eccentric and unknowable friend.

We finished our second year of college and got jobs during the summer to save some money. We both found it hard to stay put that spring and summer. I remember being out late one night with Thad, walking down the street, restless and horny, and Thad suddenly said, There's not a man in this whole town that can fuck me as hard as I need to get fucked. I had tried, but Thad needed a bigger, meaner man than I was. After we'd been in New York for a couple of years and had split up, I would see Thad occasionally at sex clubs and the sauna, always alone, tattooed, and looking like a hungry, wounded, feral animal. I saw him again recently, looking the same way. He pretended not to recognize me. I don't know why.

AIDS was at its most rampant and terrifying when I arrived in New York. Many of the people I met had contracted HIV before they knew how to prevent it, and the treatments at the time were primitive compared to what is available now. I met a poet named Gerard who lived on Staten Island, and I spent a whole winter going back and forth on the ferry to see him. He lived in a large house with some other people; they were all Buddhists and hippies, gentle and kind and a little odd. I didn't know it, but Gerard had AIDS.

Gerard was always more careful than I to make sure that the sex we had was safe—if he hadn't been I would probably not be HIV-negative, as I still am. I don't know when he found out about his disease, but he told me about it only after we had long broken up and he was getting very sick. Then we became close again, and I was with him when he died. He had surrounded himself with a large group of people devoted to New Age beliefs and Marianne Williamson's *Course in Miracles*. I found most of these people and their cheerful religion hard to take. I resented their insipid congratulations to Gerard for the wonderful journey into the light he was about to take. My kind of grief was closer to the way Gerard's mother felt, and the two of us would cry together out in the hallway of the hospital while the others laughed and celebrated with Gerard in his room. I suppose they were doing their best, but Gerard's death was sadder for me than it might have been—and for him, too, I believe—because of their perverse denial of its tragic aspect. New York, after that, was different for me, because I was different: I'd seen AIDS and death up close and I had lost someone I loved.

But my life went on, and it kept on changing. I worked for several years as an editorial assistant at a big publishing house, and I studied poetry at NYU. I remember Harold Bloom reading aloud a cool poem by Wallace Stevens and crying over it by the end, teaching his graduate students the connection between beauty and feeling in a few memorable minutes; I'd never learned so much so fast. I quit my job to go back to school full-time, and I got a degree in philosophy. I worked part-time as managing editor of an academic journal, and went to Paris for five summers to work in a small music library. But mostly I stayed in New York and went about my business. I wrote a novel and dance reviews and book reviews and I tried to figure out what to do with myself. I never did succeed in figuring it out, though, and I still have no very clear idea about what I will do in the future.

છે

How did I come to prostitution? Of course there is no single answer. The answer, in fact, cannot be reduced to anything less than a view of my whole life: the sadnesses, the rebellions, the loneliness, the joie de vivre, the bad childhood and the teenage misery and the relative happiness of being a young man in the city—it is all relevant. Having sex with men for money is something I did for a while. It was an interesting experience, but not, in itself, nearly so interesting as life is for me now, with its subtle play of tension and relief, its moral quandaries and occasional epiphanies. I was addicted for years to drugs, drinking, and sex; the combined effect of these addictions gave me a degree of freedom from reality; it also prevented me from any sort of spiritual or moral growth. Life as an addict and a hustler was static and repetitive; now it is less predictable and something I care much more about.

What brought me to New York was a long, tortuous road, dangerous and exciting. I have had the time of my life in the city; I have also had some of my darkest hours here. The perplexing thing is that the best and the worst of times for me—when I felt that I was living full-out and with real ferocity, but also suffering from a crisis of hopelessness—were almost simultaneous. I was wildly alive and nearly dead at the very same time.

21 November 96

Last night I slept with John C. It was lovely fucking him and kissing him again and then sleeping with him in his bed, with all his high-intellectual books around. This morning he got up and put on a suit and Gucci loafers and I walked him to work. During the brief, fitful sleep, I had a very strong dream: I was making love to my dad in a living room when my mom came in unexpectedly and found me sucking his dick. She said, "What is the matter with you? Sucking your father's cock!" She was furious, and began storming around the house. I had an insatiable lust for his dick—it was large and hard and tasted good and I wanted him to fuck me and I was upset that she had come home and interrupted what I was experiencing as a kind of consummation. During the sex with him, I was very happy and my sexual hunger was being dealt with in what felt like a very good way. Something about his cock in particular was very attractive to me. The dream makes me extremely uncomfortable, partly because of the purity and completeness of my attraction to my dad and his cock. What does it mean? I woke up feeling very exhilarated and happy.

24 November 96

Hung over. Another ridiculous night out. Started off nicely, going with Charles to Steve B.'s birthday party, where I saw

Brett, who was cool and beautiful as usual. Then Charles and I went off to bars and began the evening's coke. I got paged and went to work and then ended up at Club 82, had some sex, etc. The usual. Was hoping John would call, but he didn't. Came home at 4:30. Still reeling from the dream about my dad—it feels as if the dream had some kind of serious effect on me sexually. I still don't know what it's all about. Maybe it clarified something for me. I feel . . . susceptible. To what? Betsy called drunk and funny from London.

25 November 96

Toby was operated on today. The surgeon said it went well though he lost two pints of blood. I seem to have no boyfriend prospects at the moment, and I'm living the life of a whore. Listening to Offenbach overtures and trying to write. 3:45 A.M. Back from Chelsea bars on a Monday night. Jesus. Confusing, my life. Ran into a bartender I know who reminded me of his name, but I've already forgotten it again, and I might see him later yet tonight. Doing coke all night. I seem to be in the middle of an extraordinary phase in my life. I'm not sure what to do—is it okay? Am I wasting my life? Does it matter?

26 November 96

Survived last night. Went out again at 4:30 to meet Claudio, the bartender, and came home again at 7 this morning. At 12:30 I called Jonathan and cancelled lunch. I finally managed to get to New York Hospital at 4:30 to see Toby, who was not looking very well, still in the recovery room more than twenty-four hours after the operation, and he's staying there again tonight.

27 November 96

Saw Toby, who was hallucinating and bored but recovering pretty well, I think. Very pleasant visit. Saw Hitchcock's Lifeboat *last night. Tallulah Bankhead was a great old movie star; the only role she ever played was T.B. playing a character in a movie. Living in a certain theatrical mode.*

15 December 96

Saw Betsy last night. We drank until 3 and then I came home. No work from Big Guns, and I owe them $100. I have $34 in the bank and less than a hundred in cash. I guess this is when I'm supposed to admit that my drug habit has become a problem. But I'll admit nothing!

19 December 96

*I have too little money, I'm getting too little work from Big
Guns, and I can't concentrate. I'm addicted to sex and
cocaine—well, if not addicted, since Betsy hates to hear me say
that, then* habituated *to them, then—and I haven't been to
sleep before 5 A.M. in weeks. But I wouldn't want to complain,
or to become "too depressed to savor my melancholia."*

20 December 96

*Last night I did a job for Big Guns, spent four hours with
W. L., a perfectly nice middle-aged man who wanted to do a
great deal of cocaine and then roll around on the bed. It was
very easy, and the coke made the time fly, and I came away
having made $600. A.M. called to invite me to dinner, but I
said I couldn't go. I just don't feel up to it.*

21 December 96

*A very Rimbaud day—a Rimbaud period, relatively late in
my life, given R.'s integration of his own hell by nineteen, and
his renunciation of making anything of it thereafter. But then,
maybe we're living in a kind of time in which hell comes late—
it gets deferred longer now. Last night was hell for me. I was
home until 11:30, then went out for no reason whatever, to
Characters to buy coke, where I met Noel, a beautiful young*

man who flirted with me for about ten minutes and then flirted with everyone else. I went to the East Village, to Club 82 of course, where I met David, who turned out to be a hair colorist and a nightmare. I knew it right away, but for some perverse reason I went home with him anyway and eventually, after he said he'd just tested negative for HIV last week, I let him fuck me without a rubber. My ass was very tight, and the whole thing was painful and nasty. My behavior was being dictated by some pretty ugly instincts, and I left his apartment this morning feeling nearly ill. I slept until 3:00 P.M., then went downtown to get paid for the other night's job. I'm trying to stay home tonight for the first time in ages. I feel afraid of myself. Rimbaud: "Finally I learned to consider sacred the very disorder of my mind." And Pascal: "I strive only to know my nothingness." And Seidel: "I rot before I ripen."

23 December 96

Woke up to a phone call from Ian, the wild drag agent, asking if I could do a call at 2:30 this afternoon. I went. He was a pretty attractive thirtyish Hawaiian guy en route to Europe. We talked about getting together again tonight. Later I went downtown to deliver some money to Ian and met Damian, a cute boy working in a T-shirt shop on Christopher Street. May see him later too. At lunch I saw John M., a young actor I saw in a play last *month. I liked him in the play and I liked him today. We too exchanged, as Charles would say, vital statistics. Bought a coat for Mom and some other junk for the others. Home tomorrow, then to Atlanta for the philosophy conference.*

30 December 96

Just back from Ohio and Atlanta. Mom and Chris were late to pick me up at the airport, but not too late, and she seemed happy to see me, as I was to see her. She looked about the same, and so did Chris. It's obvious to probably everyone that Mom is not at all in love with him, but nonetheless it looks like a decent marriage and I believe it has a chance of lasting—if Mom can have an affair with someone that turns her on without divorcing Chris. At home, Liz, Jenni, and Mike with his pregnant new wife, and later his daughter, a very cute five-year-old who seemed to like me. I liked her, too, and was glad that I'd brought her a nice little leather jacket for Xmas, which she loved. Liz finished a semester of school with Bs, but seemed depressed and drinks too much. She has a boyfriend who's an angel, though I suspect that if he followed her to NYC, she'd get tired of him as she did the last guy. Our family curse. She says she's coming back to New York in February. I spent a lot of time with her in her little apartment above Mom's store. I love Liz so much, and we became a little closer while I was there, so that now we are very close indeed. Not only do I love her, but I like her as a friend, and would like her to be around as much as she would like. The whole Xmas thing was bearable, sometimes even pleasant, though it was no more fun than it's ever been to see most of the extended family. On coke the whole time, of course. After Xmas I went to Atlanta for the philosophy conference. Met Taylor L., a 6'4" twenty-three-year-old boy, and we had some fun together. The second night we met a hustler in a bar, though we weren't sure what he was until we were all in Taylor's apartment. The hustler said he had a fourteen-year-old boyfriend at home. We had some good three-way sex (for free) and then the hustler drove off in his truck, back to his child lover. Found a copy of Ronald Firbank's Collected Stories *at a bizarre little bookshop. I look forward to "Lady Appledore's Mesalliance." If only I could calm down long enough to read something.*

1 January 97

Spent New Year's Eve with Damian and went to a party near Times Square—quite a good party, lots of confetti, sillier and more impressive than I expected. Reading a good book about psychology by Drury, a student of Wittgenstein's. He quotes a wonderful letter from Simone Weil to a student in which she advises the student to avoid living for sensation, to develop rather a quiet inner life, and to avoid love, to play sports, and go hiking in the mountains—good advice, and a good example of what Drury means by the further reaches of psychology's usefulness. For my part, of course, I am addicted to sensation in all of its seductive variety, and my inner life of late has been far back in the back of my head, hiding in shame. I can only hope it will come out again when I finally decide to ease up on giving it such good reasons to be ashamed. In other words, when I get stronger, or more spiritually "hygienic" to quote, of all people, Gordon.

3 January 97

Very, very strange days. Spent a night with Brett—I gave him my Prada sweater and he gave me a book about Yvonne Rainer and a beautiful thick silver chain of his I've long admired. Then we snorted some heroin and had very good, long-lasting sex. Then, at about 4:30 A.M., we heard fire trucks outside and found that the building next to his was on fire. We woke up the people on his floor and went downstairs. On the way down, I looked out the window and saw that the top two floors were in bright orange flames, and a man was hanging from the top-floor window. When I got to the next floor down, he wasn't there anymore. Out on the street, we eventually saw the guy carried by on a stretcher, demolished and bloody. I heard someone say that he'd fallen eight floors, so I sat down and vomited. All in all I had a great time with B. and I've been thinking vague thoughts about him ever since. Last night I found myself once again in his neighborhood, and I thought of calling him, but went to Club 82 instead and wished I was with him. Tonight is dinner with Charles and then Squeeze Box on X—that's the plan. What a mess my life has become. And yet I feel somehow almost happy, almost giddy with happiness of a sort. I feel alive, I guess—as if liveliness is doing a good job at doing something or another for me. Probably disguising a profound depression, etc. etc. But fuck it.

4 January 97

Picked up a decorator from Squeeze Box last night and brought him here, then kicked him out after about an hour. To sleep at 7. Thought about Brett. Wondering if I should try to see him tonight. No work from the agency since I got back to town, and Malaga sent rejection notes today from Harper's *of the hustling piece and from* Crown *of the novel—an ugly little ungrammatical thing it is, too. This from a book editor: "the 'operatic' tone of the novel seems to me more baroque and not to my taste." More baroque than what, for fuck's sake?*

7 January 97

Been with Brett every night for three or four days, and every night we've snorted heroin and then had great sex and wonder-

ful conversations. I wonder how much the heroin has to do with it. His friend Peter C.'s funeral is tomorrow morning, and then I guess things will begin to get back to normal, for better or worse. I'm hustling almost every night. All very bizarre.

10 January 97

The end of a strange week spent largely with Brett and S., the boyfriend of the late Peter C., who died on Sunday at thirty-seven from a brain hemorrhage. Brett overextended himself in more ways than one: he got very little sleep over a period of several days, did his share of heroin over the same period, and had some pretty wild sex with me. Finally on Wednesday night, after the funeral that morning, he nearly collapsed. It got to be very late (about 6:00) when he began hallucinating and, whenever he relaxed, jolting violently back awake. He told me to go to sleep and he would take a shower (at about 7:00). I lay there for a while but didn't hear the shower, so I went to find him— in the kitchen, more or less deeply asleep standing up leaning against the refrigerator. I had to hold him up to get him back to bed, where he told me he felt that he was going to die. I opened the window to get some air, and eventually he lay down and finally fell asleep after my command that he sleep or I call 911. He assured me that he hadn't taken too much dope—I don't know what a heroin overdose looks like, after all, since I wasn't able to see myself the night I took too much. The general situation between us seems to have reverted more or less back to its usual chaos, with neither of us sure what the other is thinking, etc. And of course the problem stems, as always, from the fact that I don't know what I want. I have had a good time with him lately, though I don't feel any strong inclination to see him again right now, which he must know—he was very cool on the phone tonight. Back home last night I phoned the agency to say I wanted to go to bed and not work, but Jim said he was still hopeful about a job he'd mentioned earlier, so I lay in bed wondering if I was going to have to go out—and finally fell asleep with no phone call. My life is pretty much as inelegant as it could possibly be.

5.

In *Sowing*, Leonard Woolf's autobiography of his childhood and Cambridge years, he wishes on page fifty-four
that he "could recall vividly what it felt like to be a boy
of twelve or thirteen." He has, he says, only "a dim
remembrance of it." Aside from some unusual "intervals
of terrific energy and high spirits," he "seemed to live in
a condition of almost suspended animation, a kind of
underwater existence.... It was a dream world.... I
wanted to wake up and, at the same time, was half afraid
of doing so. Now at the age of nearly eighty I am
doubtful whether I ever have."

I wonder if I ever will. I have had the feeling of wak-
ing up *somewhat* many times, but never completely or
permanently, and I, like Virginia Woolf's husband, am
half afraid of doing so. When I was hustling full time, I
was more fully in a dream world than I am now, certainly. This was partly due to the drugs I was on, but
partly it was a state of mind that a hustler instinctively
develops. It's nothing very mysterious; it's just a mixture
of denial, laziness, and romanticism. I read someplace
that a good definition of a romantic is someone who
always wants to be elsewhere. That's me. And when

you're a hustler, you are always elsewhere. Your mind is never where you are, and you are someplace different every hour or two anyway. Keeping your mind and your body apart is not at all hard to do: you just let yourself drift away. And it is deeply pleasurable, at least for a while. Hustling itself was not normally a pleasure for me, but I enjoyed the trance in which I lived. I don't miss that state of mind, but I could understand missing it. In any case, I have not completely woken up from it. The teacher of a meditation class I took for a while after I stopped hustling used to say that meditating was about being fully awake and "managing your energy." Practicing yoga and meditation has given me "intervals of terrific energy and high spirits," but then so has speed, the drug. The drugless intervals—when I was focused and relaxing into myself—were probably somehow more authentic and more deserved. But I am a skeptic, and I tend to believe that the most valuable, memorable, and satisfying experiences in life tend to happen mostly when we're not expecting them.

I don't think I could claim that being high on heroin or crystal meth and having sex with an undesirable stranger is far up in my hierarchy of experience, but nor would I want to say that I was more corrupted or debased by those times than I have sometimes been by society generally or certain people in particular. I can think of plenty of situations in which I was badly wounded by a group's neglect of manners and lack of kindness, and we have all been hurt by other people's cruelty even if it *was* disguised as wit. In fact, I'm sure that I was "held" in a comforting way by many of the men I was hired by as a hustler; and at many other times in my life I have needed to be held that way and have not been. I am almost completely out of touch with most of my family, for example. Even my mother almost never calls me; I call her. Tonight, I am at home alone listening to waltzes by Johann Strauss. I'm a little lonely, but I am overall pretty happy. For I, like Leonard Woolf, "feel passionately in the depths of my being that in the last resort *nothing matters*. The belief in the importance of truth and the impossibility of absolute truth, the conviction that, though things rightly matter profoundly to you and me, nothing matters—this mental and emotional metaphysic or attitude towards the universe" is of great help in sustaining this qualified and nervous happiness of mine.

✎

I have known all along that in order to write this book I would have to dredge up memories that I would really prefer not to recall. Getting on with your life, and living differently from the way you have been living, is hard enough. I'm sure that everyone forgets about some of the things they are ashamed of. I can remember, if I try to, what it was like to be with certain clients in their apartments and in their beds. I can recall something of what I felt at the time; I remember not feeling very much. I can definitely remember the cravings for drugs and sex and money. And I believe that it is good for me to write about these things, to analyze them and be clear about them, to be open and honest. I have not spent much time in my life remembering, and I know it is time for me to remember now in order to get safely past the old way of living. The fact that some part of me is resisting this process only reinforces my conviction that what I'm doing is worthwhile.

I told someone about my idea for this book before I had really begun to write it, and she said that the important thing would be to help my reader understand how I *felt* when I was hustling. She said that anybody would be interested in those feelings, and that if I could succeed at describing them, then my book would be irresistible, and would sell well. But I don't believe that feelings are the kind of thing that can be adequately described. Feelings are shown or expressed—as in music, or in a play, or as when an angry man is compelled to fight, or a sad person cries, or a happy person glows. Music can suggest feelings, and some poetry can. Walt Whitman evokes a kind of rapturous, religious feeling in almost all of his poetry, as in these lines from *Leaves of Grass*: "Unscrew the locks from the doors!/Unscrew the doors themselves from their jambs!" Whitman does not describe his feeling, but summons it, or expresses it, with a metaphor of opening up, of permanently taking away whatever threatens to close down his ecstasy. I suppose some religious writers have tried to describe a feeling like Whitman's, but I have never read a description that seemed sufficient to the feeling, as Whitman's poetry sometimes does.

Prostitution would be a complicated metaphor. Everything about it is qualified. Every positive thing is crossed by something negative, and everything really bad about it is leavened by something that is not so bad. And, of course, a hustler is compensated for his trouble. The pragmatic question is whether he is compensated well enough. But if I believed that the money I was making as a hustler were sufficient compensation, of course, I would still be hustling.

One aspect of hustling that might be used as a
metaphor is the fact that a hustler is always expected to
comply, to some extent, with his client's wishes. That
specific submission could represent what a person does
for someone else over a longer period of time, as in a
marriage, in an atmosphere of assumed intimacy. A
hustler, for example, might suck his client's dick just
because that is what the client wants; and a wife might
submit to her husband's wishes in a similar way (or the
husband might be submissive to his wife) in exchange
for tranquility or companionship or even money itself.
But then thinking of hustling in that way might be a
case of simply calling one thing by the name of something else: being a hustler is surely completely different
in quality from being a spouse. But one way to allevi-
ate the boredom of hustling is to think of a session
with a client as a dramatic situation—to appreciate the
conflict. And the relationship of a hustler to a client is
never just one of friendliness, let alone love; real
friends don't buy or sell their favors, they just give
them away. Often, though—again, as in many mar-
riages—the conflict is deeply hidden. On the surface, a
good escort persuades his client that their relationship
is real, affectionate, and sexy.

In John Preston's 1994 *Hustling: A Gentleman's Guide to the Fine Art of Homosexual Prostitution*, he says "every man has something about him that is attractive and sexy. *Every man*." With a few notable exceptions, I have found that to be true. Trying to appreciate a thing is a good way to find that thing's best qualities, and men are things, especially to a hustler. Many men are heroic in their refusal to be pathetic, and hustlers are sometimes the only people to get a glimpse of a man in his loneliness, or in the weakness of his desire. And it is sometimes only by seeing this contrast—of a man on his knees who is normally an image of strength—that we can perceive the heroic aspect.

❧

One night I got a call from the agency at about midnight. I was told to plan on being busy for several hours at least. The client had a reputation for keeping his hustlers long into the night, and he would pay by check later in the week—he had a standing arrangement with the agency. I arrived at his apartment around 1:00 A.M. on a weeknight, ready for anything. I had a good supply of crystal meth, and I was feeling fine.

Martin, the client, was the only child of a rich
banker, and his parents had both died, leaving him a
huge fortune: this I learned from my agent. Martin told
me that he had spent his whole life in search of a good
time, and he considered himself a connoisseur of sex
and fun. He kept a large stash of cocaine in a handsome
wood box on the table in his living room, and a few
minutes after I arrived we began snorting it. Martin
struck me as a man who had had to fight vigorously
against himself for the self-confidence he was now able
to exhibit with a degree of pride; he seemed emotionally delicate in a way I have noticed certain other
wealthy people to be, as if his composure was well made
but thin and breakable. He seemed a person who
thought of himself as rich and spoiled, and amusing, but
otherwise not of much interest to the world, nor of any
extraordinary value. His apartment was nicer than most
johns', and his taste in paintings was really good. But he
had an unfortunate passion for late-twentieth-century
musicals, and the record he was listening to when I got
there was awful.

After a little while, Martin started getting aroused, and
he began to remove my clothes. I drew out the striptease,
and lingered in my jeans, moving away from Martin,

shirtless and seductive. At the time, I was in good shape
and rather proud of my body; I always liked to step away
from a client at some point and give him the opportunity to take a good look at me. I smoked a cigarette and I
did some more of Martin's excellent coke. I changed the
dreadful music to something more innocuous. I opened
a bottle of Martin's very good wine in the kitchen, and
went to the bathroom for another big bump of speed.

We eventually landed on Martin's bed and wrestled
around there, which my agent had told me was Martin's
favorite thing to do (he likes to win *and* lose, the agent
had said).

At about 3:00 A.M., during a break, I asked Martin if
he'd ever hired two hustlers at once. Of course he had,
he said, and he loved it. I said I thought it would be a
good time, and Martin reached for the phone. So call
your agent, he said, and see if they can send someone
over. Of course they could.

Martin had already been with Francisco several times
before, and he was pleased with the agent's suggestion.
When Francisco came into Martin's bedroom I was very
high and deeply involved with a porno movie, but
Francisco smelled as good as he looked. He was Hispanic,
with his dark hair pulled back, and a beautiful, dark body,

which he too revealed slowly and at some distance from Martin and me. Francisco was relaxed and ready to stay for a long, long time, and he seemed to like me. It was 4:30 A.M., and the party had apparently just begun.

I mentioned to Francisco and Martin that I had some crystal meth and that they were welcome to have some; they both accepted. The three of us were aware that snorting this drug would complement the cocaine and drive us on well into the morning. Francisco and I were happy to stay for the money—we were both making at least $150 an hour and the agency was now making $200, which would make them happy. And Martin was the kind of guy who liked to stay up having sex all night regardless of the expense or the consequences. His maid was due at 9:00 A.M. and he was expected at brunch with some friends the next day; he said, with a grin, that he would just pay the maid and tell her to go home and he would cancel the brunch. So we were all gladly determined to keep things going indefinitely.

Francisco—who subsequently became a kind of occasional partner of mine whenever either of us needed a second hustler for a client (and sometimes just for fun)—was extremely good at his job. He gave me an intense education that night: to my surprise, he treated

Martin as a god. He persuaded Martin (who was in his late forties and not in great shape, and in any case was in possession of neither great beauty nor charm) that he, Francisco, really found Martin deeply attractive and sexy, and Francisco seemed almost to believe it himself. He kissed Martin passionately and handled him familiarly, like a lover. He sucked Martin's small, flaccid dick, and seemed to love it. And he took full advantage of my presence to give Martin an erotic show. Francisco and I went round and round, kissing and sucking each other's cocks and fucking each other with abandon. We both liked to play rough, and Martin liked to watch rough— the rougher the better, as he said. We kept drinking Martin's wine, snorting his coke and my crystal, pausing to watch porno movies, kissing and fondling Martin, and fucking each other madly, slapping each other around, and wrecking Martin's bedroom with cast-off condoms, lubricant wiped on the bed, spilled wine and empty little bottles that had been full of white powders. I had never been involved in anything on quite this scale before. The sun came up outside, so we shut the curtains. The three of us took a shower at 8:00 o'clock and I assumed that we were finished. But Francisco was clever, and his capacity for sex was evidently enormous.

He ended up lying in the bathtub while Martin and I
pissed on him, and the trick worked: Martin was ready
for more, and we dried off quickly and went back to
bed. When the maid rang the doorbell, Martin sent her
home. I was astonished by all of this and beginning to
get seriously restless; but I reminded myself that I was
making amazing money, and somehow I got yet another
hard-on. Money really can be an aphrodisiac.

In the hours leading up to noon, the sex got to be
pretty much beside the point. The whole idea by then, I
believe, was just not to be alone and awake at the same
time, and none of us could sleep. We listened to music
and talked. Martin began to show little signs of irrita-
tion, as if he was beginning to realize the extent of what
we all had done. He'd missed his lunch date. His room
was a mess, his wine was all gone, he was down to a
mere few bottles of coke, and we were still there, taking
his money—and yet he didn't want us to leave.

But around noon, we showered again and finally put
on some clothes for warmth. We put Martin to bed, and
Francisco and I slipped out the door and into the blaz-
ing sunlight. It was warm and humid outside; it was a
weekday in Manhattan. I have never felt stranger than I
did walking along the street that day in midtown. I had

had sex for eleven hours. I was drunk, high, hungry, and exhausted. Francisco, who seemed totally unbothered by his only slightly shorter go-round with me and Martin, suggested that we get bagels and go up to his nearby roof and lie in the sun to sleep. We were almost dangerously horny.

On Francisco's rooftop, the heat from the sun was fierce. I couldn't eat, and could barely move at all. I was impressed that Francisco was in such good condition. He happily soaked up the sun and stretched his muscles. He ate his bagel and then he ate mine. He figured out how much money poor Martin had spent on the two of us—about $3800, which did not seem like an extraordinary amount to Francisco. He said that he had once spent an entire weekend with Martin on Fire Island and made $5000 himself. He told me that he really liked Martin, and he implied that the affection he displayed for Martin in bed was completely real, which I said I found hard to believe. What's to like so much? I asked him. He's an unremarkable man who sits around listening to Andrew Lloyd Weber musicals when he's not too busy drinking, snorting coke, and paying for sex. Or buying beautiful Japanese paintings, Francisco said, or reading good books, or talking with his interesting friends, or cooking really good food. I've known Martin for a long time, he said. I've watched him get older and thinner, and I'll probably see him die—you know he's HIV positive, don't you? He might not be my first choice for a lover, Francisco said, but he wouldn't be my last choice in the world, either.

You're new to this, he said. You can still be tough. But eventually working is just a part of your life, and johns are just people you get to know. I don't like to take any-body's money unless I give him something equally valu-able in exchange. They can feel it if you're faking it. Don't fake it. Why should you? It doesn't cost you any-thing to feel it, but if you have sex with people for a long time without giving them anything but sex, that will hurt you eventually. Nobody can do that for long.

Francisco, in his Versace underwear and dark glasses, tilted back his head so that the sun was on his face. He seemed at home surrounded as he was by tall buildings and blaring traffic down in the street, as if the beach were in his head and that's the way he liked it.

That afternoon any feelings I had were large, slow-moving things that were just there, without making much impact or doing much damage. Eventually Francisco and I went into his bedroom and lay down. We fucked again, to relax (Francisco said), and then went to sleep. I felt close to Francisco, and we agreed to be friends.

Unfortunately though, and it probably is my fault, Francisco and I have not become friends after all. While *he* seemed able to let experiences like the one we shared at Martin's apartment more or less roll off his back, and not to be upset by them, I was not so resilient. Francisco had been hustling a lot longer than I had been, and he had apparently learned how to stay connected to himself and to his feelings regardless of what he saw or did. I really liked him, and respected him. But I knew that doing what I was doing was making me immune to almost any feelings at all. I had unconsciously learned not to feel what an experience would in the past have caused me to feel. My defenses were becoming my personality—and I needed my defenses if I were to keep hustling, which Francisco himself had pointed out to me on his roof. Francisco was somehow able to think of his clients as people, whereas I inevitably thought of them as examples of something like waywardness. I couldn't bear to see clearly just what they were—lonely at least, often really unhappy or worse—and my feelings about these men were controlled to the point of ceasing to exist. Francisco's capacity to feel close to his clients made me queasy and suspicious and sad: how could he cope with all of those feelings? I didn't understand, and I was depressed by Francisco's toughness, if that's what it was. Eventually I found it impossible to be the friend of someone so committed to other people's loneliness. While I was hustling I preferred to hold myself in a condition of ignorance, to sustain my dreamlike state for as long as it would last.

No work lately from the agency, and Malaga, at the other agency, is on vacation, so no news from her. I should try to appreciate this quiet time, I know, but on the other hand my life is pretty static right now—no money, no progress, not much art or sex. I've more or less decided to begin the new novel yet again. Brett read it and liked it, but said that it certainly is not "light," and it would be better if it were, with which I agree. I think I should try the experiment of really trying to work friv-olously (I'm not even sure how to spell that word!), taking Firbank as my model—trying to make myself giddy with silli-ness. Because I feel sure that such a technique could produce a really profound novel. Do I believe that? Yes, I do. Because the long pursuit of a good, fun, silly time is a profound, true-to-life emotional situation for people—certainly for me.

Yesterday worked for the agency, in Queens. A middle-aged Catholic guy, very ordinary, very weird. Then to dinner at F.'s with Toby. Then to Brett's, whence Joey and I went out to cop dope on the street—the last time I'll do that, because it was too scary for my delicate disposition. Long, intense night with B. Today to the gym with Liz, where I changed my membership to a family one to include her, and I bought her a pair of boots.

I'm so happy to have my little sister living with me. She's adorable. I have to wonder what she thinks I do all night. Does she think I'm just out with friends at bars and clubs? I'm sure, regardless of what she thinks, that I'm not setting a very good example for her.

24 January 97

No work lately from Big Guns—a little worrisome, since I definitely need some money coming in additional to the little Forum *salary. And I'll also need some kind of real job this summer.*

26 January 97

Nice night with B., Joey, and Ornell, Joey's boyfriend. We watched the original The Fly *and then we drove to White Castle in Queens for a lark, and to the Bar, etc. No plans for tonight except once again to try, without much confidence, to write. Last night when I arrived at B.'s, he talked about feeling strung out (from dope). As I told Charles, all my feelings about him and the situation are unclear, but I do have a good time with him and don't much miss promiscuity. Though I suppose a part of me does. I don't know much of anything anymore, and I feel heavy and tired.*

30 January 97

To Brett's for pasta last night, then worked—for Jack T., a very nice old guy, and quite sexy, though a bit of a cheapskate. Back to B.'s, and Joey and I went out to cop dope again and got beat—nothing but baking soda. B. gave me a little of what he had left, so I got a little high, we watched The Anniversary, *a disgusting movie with Bette Davis, and went to sleep, no sex. After work at the* Forum, *went to Club Monaco and stole a pair of pants and bought a shirt and tie. First time I've shoplifted from a big NYC store like that, where the security is supposedly tight. Ha. Quite nerve-wracking and heady.*

3 February 97

Brett and I planning a trip to Niagara Falls, maybe this week-end, with Joey and Ornell.

5 February 97

Watched Niagara, *the movie, with Brett. Then we argued when I said something about needing to get a job, or make some kind of real change—complaining about my lack of success, etc. He called me a brat, and said I don't want to work but just have everything handed to me. It was an odd conversation, and we went to sleep on separate sides of his bed. This morning*

I went to work at the Forum and looked in the Voice for a job. Off to a party with Melinda D.

7 *February 97*

Accepted a job yesterday as assistant to John C. I begin two weeks from Monday. I gave two weeks' notice at the Forum this morning. I'll go to Santa Fe on May 5 and stay there all summer. I'm very confused.

15 *February 97*

Brett says Friday will make five years that we've known each other. What a complicated relationship we have—because we love each other, no doubt.

6.

Almost every night when I was hustling full-time, I
found it impossible to go directly home after doing a job,
even if the job ended very late. I needed the promise of
good sex and some relaxation in a club or bar to look
forward to while I was with a client, and I found it somehow appropriate to get away from the man I'd been with
only to spend at least a portion of the money he'd given
me on frivolous things—taxis, drinks, and drugs. It made
the whole thing seem fun—or funner. Usually, to be
honest, it was not much fun. By the time I was finished
with work I was usually tired, high, sexually spent or fed
up, and jittery from coke or speed or both. A part of me
always wanted to go home to bed, but that part almost
never prevailed, because another part knew that being at
home alone, still cranked, was a dangerous proposition. I
still find it hard to spend a whole evening at home alone.

Fortunately, though, there is a loose, discreet society of
hustlers, drug addicts, bartenders, insomniacs, and indefati-
gable romantics in New York that convenes every night,
very late, in various after-hour bars, restaurants, and clubs.
Being a part of this scene had, for me, a certain glamour
with which a nine-to-five job, however important, could

never compare. It may seem a false and empty, even depressing, glamour; but I believe I will always remember those late, late nights downtown—5:00 A.M. on a Wednesday morning at Jay's, for example—with pleasure.

Jay's, a club in the West Village, has been slightly different things at different times for years, but in my time there it was always a place to go late at night for sex and companionship when nothing else was open. Jay's was always open, and there was always a terrific mixture of types hanging around—leathermen, drag queens, DJs, drug addicts, tourists, horny young men, and kids with energy to burn. It was as unpretentious as it could possibly have been, and it didn't seem odd to anyone there to be looking for something to do at 6:00 in the morning during the week. Downstairs there was sex, and upstairs there were porno movies, a pool table, and a pinball machine. The bar served orange juice and club soda, and everyone was smoking something. You could pretty much say anything to anyone at Jay's and he would generally say something back to you, and you never knew what he would say. There was a long line for the single stall in the bathroom, but if you were just snorting or smoking something you could do it anywhere.

Drugs have sometimes been a problem for me. The

drug I have had the most serious problem with, crystal meth, removes all sense of tiredness and makes sleep altogether impossible for about eight hours. Crystal deepens the craving and prolongs the capacity for sex. It also tends to exacerbate mood swings, and after a few sleepless days and nights it can make you feel seriously crazy. I was addicted to crystal for about four months toward the end of the time I spent working full-time as a hustler; I snorted it several times a day, every day. During this period I slept badly, when I slept, for a few hours at a time, after several—sometimes six or eight—exquisitely torturous hours of masturbation with my VCR. Some of the sex I had on crystal—mostly at the sauna—was unsafe. If I wasn't ecstatic, I was miserable. It was the only time in my life as an adult that I felt sinful—not for having sinned against God, but for having given up my own principles. I had always felt that I could change any specific thing about myself if I really wanted to—that I could stop, or slow down, or switch to something else. But not when I was addicted to speed.

I took crystal meth for the first time because that's what the dealer was selling—I was looking for coke. He said it would keep me awake, and that's what I wanted at the time above all else. I wanted to stay awake in order

to have more fun (I was at the sauna and had just got
back to town after four months away). The speed did
keep me awake, and it was smoother than coke, and I
could keep a hard-on, and I wanted to fuck again after
I'd come twice, and it didn't make me jittery. It did
exactly what I wanted it to do. Speed stimulates the
pleasure center of the brain; it makes everything feel
better and it makes some things, like fucking and getting
fucked, feel really, really good for a long time (if you're
lucky enough to have the right partner, or a sufficient
supply of them). Your body gives you no sign that you
should stop—ever. There were times when I went for
days without any sleep, doing little more than fucking
and beating off—for money, for free, for lack of anything better to do, and because I just couldn't stop.

It was a bad time. I felt as if my life was completely
out of my control, and I thought I would end up dead
from exhaustion or suicide. Yet I can't say that I regret
having taken the drug: never before or since have I felt
quite equal to the force of all of my desires.

Eventually while I was still hustling I forced myself to
stop buying crystal and returned to cocaine, a cheaper,
more banal drug, but one which provides the kind of
quick rush that prevents the experience of hustling (or

anything else) from feeling too grim. When I stopped hustling, I stopped using coke, too. A couple of months later I bought some crystal again, and I made the tiny $50 supply last a week. It was a lot of fun, and I'm not sorry I did it again, and I know that the only reason I don't have any right now is that it is hard to find and expensive. My old dealer is a wanderer, and he never answers his phone. He's someone I used to run into at the sauna, and sometimes he would call if I paged him. If I saw him tonight, I would probably buy some speed if I had the money. That's what being clean means for me for now: making an effort to accept my dealer's evasiveness and my favorite drug's inaccessibility.

∽

It's not difficult for a hustler to have strictly safe sex, at least when he's hustling. My friends often cringed with worry when they heard I was working, but the temptation of unsafe sex is more a result of addiction to sex than getting paid for it. Unfortunately, in my case at least the two tended to go hand in hand. I don't believe I could have worked as an escort if I didn't have an inclination to promiscuity. I may not often have been excited by my clients, but I do need a great deal of sexual attention, and most of my clients were excited by me. I have no real complaint about having a strong sex drive, but the more sex I have, the more I need, and hustling tends to up the sexual ante, not because the sex is good (though sometimes it is), but just because it's sex.

The money, of course, is the trump. An escort is always paid in untaxed cash, and I almost never worked for less than $150 an hour. There is a lot to be said for going around the city with four or five hundred dollars in large bills, and this aspect of hustling was thrilling, at least for someone such as myself who has never had much money.

The most interesting aspect of prostitution, however, was the furtive meeting with clients. Most of the jobs I did were with men I had never met before and would never see again. The experience was always different, in the details, from anything I had ever known, and hustling gave me glimpses—and sometimes longer looks—into the private lives of many men, which aside from being useful to me as a writer was fascinating to me as a human being. If hell is other people, I like to think that the time I spent with all those men, and their often bizarre idiosyncrasies, gave me some knowledge that, if only by way of contrast, hints at some of the qualities of heaven.

જી

One of the last hustling jobs I did was on a Sunday afternoon. I was working for myself, advertising on a phone line. When I was paged, I was in the middle of a poker game and didn't return the call for nearly an hour. When I did, an answering machine came on with a greeting from a doctor's office. I decided to go ahead and leave a message since I had nothing to lose, and when I began to speak, the doctor himself picked up the phone and fumbled around with turning off the machine. When he finally spoke, he sounded confused and incoherent, and he asked me to hold on for a few minutes. When he finally returned to the phone, he asked me to describe myself again, and then he asked if I liked to "party." I said that I did. I asked what he had, and he said it was to smoke, but not grass, which I knew meant freebasing cocaine (or smoking crack)—this explained his condition: he was very high already. I said I would be happy to smoke up with him. He asked if my rate could be lowered in exchange for drugs, and I

agreed to a small discount. At about 6:30 P.M. we agreed
to meet at his office, which he said was "very comfortable," at midnight. He was to page me again at 11:00 to
confirm. I asked him why it would have to be so late,
and he replied that he had some work to do. I suspect
that he was with another hustler when I called.

At 11:15 I phoned the doctor again. He said he had
taken down the wrong number for my pager and was
glad I called. He asked if we could postpone our meeting until 12:30 because he wanted to finish the work he
was doing. He gave me his address, on a particularly nice
block in the Village, and he told me to go down the outside steps to the basement where he would be watching
for me from the window of his office.

I arrived precisely on time, and the doctor came to
the door almost immediately, before I had even rung the
bell. He was a balding, somewhat overweight, nervous
man in his early forties. He was wearing a sweatsuit and
no shoes, and he seemed quite frantic. We entered his
office, and I discovered that he was a shrink (his word).
He said he just needed to do one thing before he could
relax, which was to cover the window, which faced the
concrete wall of the outside stairwell and was already
covered by a solid blind, with a misshapen piece of fab-

ric. He attached the fabric to the wall using a large roll of plastic tape. It was an awkward, sloppy job, and I couldn't help but find the doctor pathetic, straining to reach the top of the window for no good reason except the consolation of his irrational paranoia, his big, hairy belly showing beneath his soiled sweatshirt.

Having attached the fabric to the window, the doctor asked if we should attend to business first. Everything about him made me think of drugs, and that's what I thought he meant since he was holding a glass pipe and grinning, so I said sure. But he meant money, and I said that that could wait until later. I never did like to deal with money up front, and it was always a mistake not to, as it was here. Had I accepted his money at the beginning, I would have known the doctor didn't have enough cash to pay me to stay for nearly as long as I did.

The doctor then produced several more glass pipes, a large chunk of pure cocaine, and a lighter in the form of a small black torch that shot out a wicked little blue flame with a nasty hiss at the click of a small steel trigger. I had smoked cocaine before (with clients) and had never felt much from it. The doctor assured me that I had simply not smoked enough of it to get high. Over the course of the nearly two hours I was there with the doctor, the two of us smoked all of the coke he had, which was a lot, and we both got extremely high. He told me that when I had returned his page that afternoon he had just smoked some, and he asked at that point (and many times later) if we could get together and do the same thing again the next day. I said I would gladly come back, which was a lie. Then the doctor noticed that a small corner of the window in his office was left uncovered by the fabric he had taped up. He said he really could not bear that, and he looked around for something else he could tape up to cover the corner. He found a green garbage bag and tore it open. Again he tore off strips of tape and reached up to attach the garbage bag, which throughout the session flapped gently from a breeze in the room.

I was a little uncomfortable with the amount of time all this was taking, so I began to remove some clothes, and the doctor responded, and things began moving along. But every thirty or forty seconds the doctor would be distracted, either by his desire to smoke more cocaine or to ask again if I would come back the next day, and always—always—by his fears about what might be lurking outside the window. So we would have to stop what we were doing and one of us would peek out the window to make sure there was no one standing out there trying to discover the doctor in his guiltiness.

The doctor had mentioned that he had a boyfriend at home, which was his explanation for using his office for our rendezvous; but when I asked if he was worried about the boyfriend showing up, he said he wasn't concerned about that at all, that the boyfriend was definitely home asleep. I believed him. I asked who he thought might show up at the window on this extremely early Monday morning, and he said he couldn't think of anyone, but was simply paranoid about it, which didn't seem to strike him—a shrink—as odd or even interesting. After he'd been reassured that no one was outside the window, the doctor would once again locate the pipes, that scary little torch, and a bit of cocaine, and we would smoke again. I was shivering, and my dick had shrunk. I asked the doctor if he had any porno movies, and for the next ten minutes he went about the complicated business of turning on his television and VCR, and then the movie was some awful S and M thing that looked like some kind of weird European documentary.

Then the doctor asked if I liked Ecstasy, a drug I have occasionally taken before going to a nightclub or a party to dance all night and then have sex later: its effects tend to last for more than a few hours, and to take a good half hour to kick in. I began to think that I might make some real money off the doctor, and since I had a vague plan to go out someplace after working anyway, I was enthusiastic about having half a hit of X. But I wasn't sure why the doctor would want some, since he had said he was going home to his sleeping boyfriend as soon as we were finished. But he proceeded to look for the pill he thought he had hidden away someplace, which turned into a fruitless, fifteen-minute farce: a fat, naked doctor with a flashlight, rooting around in his cabinet, which was full of Prozac and other psychotropic drugs, porno videos, papers, knickknacks, and books, checking the window periodically, and mumbling complete nonsense. Finally he gave up the search with profuse apologies. He shouldn't have mentioned it, he said, if he didn't know where it was.

I excused myself and went in my underwear down the building's hallway to the bathroom, which was apparently shared by several offices. High as I was by then, this little foray was nerve-wracking and a little frightening for no specific reason. I did not enjoy the high from smoking cocaine. I felt very tense, and as if the inside of my body was uncontrollably sped up and nervous, my consciousness of things working far too hard. It seemed pointless and unpleasant, unlike the feeling I get from snorting the same drug, which is more like a heavy dose of short-lived and unreliable—but exciting—physical and mental energy.

I returned from the bathroom determined to shift the focus from drugs to sex in order to bring the session to an end. My resolve to stay and, presumably, earn more money, had faded due to my dislike of the drug and of the creepy doctor. I had the feeling that he was a serious drug addict and slightly crazy, perhaps as a result of the drugs. I found him completely unattractive; but I did want to get paid. In the hour or so that followed, I went through distinct, crack-fueled stages of intense boredom, hatred for the doctor, mild pleasure in fantasy, disgust with the whole sordid scenario, and concentration on getting the doctor to come so that I could get the hell out of there. Finally, with me standing over him, shouting every porn-inspired filthy line I could think of, he finished with a large, sweaty shudder. He immediately asked if I would care to stay a while longer. I said I needed to be getting along, but I said he could page me again tomorrow if he wished, and he promised that he would and that he would be sure to have some Ecstasy then.

I began to dress, and the doctor, happily spent in his leather chair—the one, I imagined, in which he sat while working with patients—said, while looking toward the dark shape of the window, without any detectable irony, in an almost childlike voice, Oh, that was wonderful! I was able to forget about the window for a while.

26 May 97, Santa Fe

Memorial Day. Lost another poker tournament at the casino. An idea for a book: an essay each on gambling, fucking, drinking, lying, cheating, hustling, drugging, stealing, speeding, and fighting.

18 July 97, still in Santa Fe

Not another fucking beautiful day! (Tim L. quoting Sarah Miles in White Mischief*).*

11 September 97, NYC

Saw Neil G. who asked what I was doing. Writing, I said. About what? he asked me. And I didn't know what to say. I want to write about something fresh, but nothing is fresh for me. Because I'm not fresh, spiritually. I think of the epigraph Toby's using for his new book, from Ivy Compton-Burnett: "'Who should like to live forever?' 'I should, provided I could have a comfortable, human life and not a spiritual one.'" All my problems, I believe, have a source in my conscience: I have guilt either for living too little or living too much, for doing bad work or none at all, etc. etc.

20 October 97

I'm addicted to crystal meth, and unhappily involved with John K., a very sweet, cute, generous man. Saw a very beautiful show of Richard Diebenkorn paintings at the Whitney. Afterward, waiting for the bus, an elegant old woman came up wearing a bright orange sweater and a red skirt. I love your outfit, I told her, and she said, Well, darling, when you're as old and rich as I am you can wear whatever you want to. Turns out she once owned a Diebenkorn. Made a lot of money selling it, too. Then I saw little Jane, Jonathan's baby girl, whom I love madly—both of them. But, oh, how little I feel—how much and how little at once. So easily bored, so hard to please, and so quickly satisfied.

7.

Occasionally Big Guns, the second agency, would send me to a client to whom I had been sent by Wow, the previous one. (And they sent me once to the ugly man who'd interviewed me for Wow, which was a pretty unpleasant surprise.) Almost invariably these clients would either not remember me or pretend not to, though a few times a man let on at the very end of the session that he had known all along that we had been together before and that he didn't mind. The agencies normally never send an escort to a man twice unless the client requests to see someone again.

One man I was sent to by Big Guns after having seen him through Wow was Jack, a very rich businessman on the Upper East Side. Jack must have been in his early seventies. I got the feeling that he was among the richest men I had ever met (and have since learned that indeed he was). He had great taste in art; he had only a few pictures, but they were all stunningly beautiful. His whole apartment was beautifully understated, deftly arranged with a few charming, lovely things. He had a real library just off the entrance to the apartment, and both times I saw him he had been sitting there, with a glass of Scotch, in his smoking jacket (though he didn't smoke). When I arrived, Jack made me a drink and got his from the library and we went into the living room, where he sat across the room from me, so that I had plenty of space and felt only the pressure of a social occasion, nothing more. Jack knew that the more space he gave me, the freer I would feel and the better I would function, both as a human being and as a sexual one. Within minutes, both times, I was completely comfortable and even glad to be where I was.

We sat talking across the room like two gentlemen in a club. He was curious to know some things about me, and he was open and interesting about himself. He was totally unashamed of his sexuality and of the situation we were in together—he was too smart for shame, and too rich. He was clearly a man who could have more or less anything he wanted, and I was something he wanted for an hour, which suited me.

In his dark bedroom, he opened the blinds to show me his view of the U.N. He seemed to consider a view of the U.N. a kind of privilege, as if he'd been cleared by security before moving into his apartment. That, too, I found charming, since a view of the U.N. is really such an unenviable thing, a fact of which Jack was perfectly well aware. He seemed amused by such ironies, and I liked his cheerfulness. Many things, for Jack, were like rather dry, grown-up jokes: nothing really mattered in the end, and most things were at least a little absurd. When I had told him a few things about my life earlier, he had taken me seriously, but hadn't hidden the fact that he was amused by such an odd story as mine. It was as if his life was *completely* different not only from mine, but from everybody's.

I found Jack, especially the second time around, very sexy. He told me that he was seventy-one years old.

In bed, he wanted a massage, and then, after ten or fifteen minutes, wanted to give me one. While massaging my back, he got aroused and said he was going to fuck me. He reached for a condom and put it on, by which time his cock had gone soft (if it had been hard), but he persisted and sort of half-fucked me, which he did with such sweetness and consideration that it felt really quite good. He came, and then I came on him. He seemed to be briefly fascinated and pleased by the little mess we had made in his very clean, orderly bedroom. He said that he'd had a wonderful time with me, and that I should take my time washing and getting dressed, and he went to his study to fetch my money. When I joined him there, he looked thoughtful, in a posture of reflection, and he was reluctant to rouse himself. He looked at me, I thought, with some kind of longing, as if we had been together a long time and he didn't want me to go—but he was resigned to saying goodbye. He gave me the money and kissed my forehead. I went out and returned to my odd, amusing life.

When I was still quite new to hustling, the first agency sent me on a call that really surprised me. The agent had described the client as an older man who had been a successful Broadway composer; I had heard of him. The man had been living in the same apartment, the agent said, in the West Forties most of his life, and it was not a fancy place by any means. But, the agent said, all he really wants to do is touch me and watch me, and I'll be out in forty minutes. Unfortunately the man was one of the agency's original customers, and they continued to give him their old rate, which meant I would make only $100. It was not a happy prospect, but the agent made it clear that I was under some obligation to go.

The agent's description of the client did not draw an

accurate picture at all. When I knocked, I heard a voice tell me to come in, so I opened the door. The apartment was a filthy, gloomy place that was crawling with cats and hadn't been cleaned in years. The old man sat in a chair in the middle of the mess, surrounded by magazines and records and books and pictures of himself and food and filth and cats. He did not appear at all clean himself, and I was immediately determined to leave straightaway. But then he spoke to me.

Aren't you a beauty! the man said, looking at me and gesturing for me to come further into the room and then to turn around for him. Oh, you are a diamond in the rough, he said. Let me just look at you.

He was silent then, looking at me from his cope of dust, the fringed and yellowed, dreary lamp next to him giving off the only light in the room.

Yes, he drawled, you are beautiful. Absolutely beautiful!

He appeared to be totally enraptured, as if he had suddenly found himself seated before the David of Michelangelo. I was impressed.

I had taken only a few steps into the room, and I didn't dare go closer to the man, but I silently removed my shirt and looked at him, hoping that I could give him a terrific orgasm by merely standing there half naked for a few moments. Almost immediately, though, I began to find the stillness of our mutual regard—and the intensity of the old man's lust—to be somehow erotic. Even his slovenliness and the ugliness and disorder of the room became suddenly touching, and I had an urge to whip the old man into a sexual frenzy. He was so modest, and his feelings and desire were completely unhidden and classic and old, as if he had been waiting for me for eighty years or more, and now he was expecting the apotheosis of his sexual life to manifest itself in his living room. I didn't know quite what to do.

The old man did not move. He did not touch himself, or stand up, or look away. I went a little closer to him, and kicked off my shoes and lit a cigarette. I looked him right in the eye and said, I'm going to fuck you like you've never been fucked before, old man. I'm going to shove this big dick of mine up your ass and fuck you til I come. This hard cock of mine is due for some hard-core sex, and you're going to give it to me right now. Are you ready for me, mister? Because I came over here to do some serious fucking, and you're the one that's going to get fucked, right now.

I still had my jeans on, and I did not have the slightest erection. My client was still seated and several feet away from me. I stood there smoking my cigarette, staring at him. I told him that I was very horny, and that I was on the verge of orgasm already. I said I had been waiting for our appointment and had resisted the urge to masturbate all day. I took another step toward him and told him to prepare himself to get fucked. I said, I'm going to let you touch my body one time, and then I'm going to fuck you like a dog. Without saying a word, he reached out his hand in my direction, and I slowly took another step closer. I said, I'm going to throw you down onto your hands and knees and rape your ass. I'm going to fuck you so hard you won't be able to sit down again. I took another step toward him, to within a few inches of his hand. I said, If you come when you touch my chest, I'm going to rape you anyway. I stood there and watched him pant. I said, You look like you need to get fucked. I leaned in and he reached out his hand and grazed my nipple, and I pulled away, and he gasped and came and moaned softly, and his hand fell away to his side. I said nothing. I put my cigarette out in an ashtray, and put on my shirt. You're a sexy guy, I said. That was very nice.

જી

I went to see a man in Chelsea, a young lawyer whose lover was out of town. This man was very accommodating—I had the feeling he would have paid double my fee if I'd asked him to. He had told the agent that he wanted to be dominated, and that he liked feet. I told the agent on the phone that I had very ugly feet, and he said not to worry, that that would make the session so much the better.

In the man's apartment, he offered immediately to remove my shoes for me, and he asked me if I would like to smoke a cigarette. He loved, he said, to be ignored. Well, I was only too happy to ignore the guy. I asked him if he had any porno movies and I asked him to make me a drink, and then I just ignored him.

We went into a sort of den where I sat in a large leather armchair smoking, drinking, watching the movie, and stroking my dick, while the lawyer kneeled before me and kept out of the way. When he blocked my view of the television screen, I would shove him down toward the floor with my feet, and he would moan. Eventually he was lying on the floor and I was standing over him. He asked if I would let him taste my toes, so I began putting my feet into his mouth, a sexual practice I had never before experienced. Once I got the hang of it and started pushing with some force, he paused to say how impressed he was that I knew how to use my feet so well. I took this as an invitation to push harder, and I began to put much of the weight of my body on his face with one of my feet and then the other, cramming my toes into the lawyer's gaping, slobbering mouth. He moaned and writhed and showed no sign of wishing to do anything different. While I watched the video and stepped on my client, I stroked my cock, more from ennui than from anything else. I found the spectacle of a hustler smushing a client's face into the floor with his feet vaguely erotic, but a little melancholy, too. The john was not at all bad looking; he was prosperous and intelligent; he had a lover and a nice apartment—I couldn't figure why he had such a strong urge to be abused. And I certainly felt invited by him to be more violent than I was.

I dated a guy for a while who liked to be beat up, or almost beat up, and I was always a little afraid of both his instinct to be hit and mine to hit him. I went through a period of wanting my lovers to be physically rough with me, but the phase came to an end when I was with a Romanian porn actor in a Paris sauna and he spit in my face and then hit me really hard while he was fucking me. I had suggested that I wanted him to behave this way with me, and he knew exactly what to do. But when he hit me that last time, it was as if he was slapping some sense into me. I realized that I'd been entertaining a death wish—some dark instinct we probably all have someplace inside of us. The lawyer on the floor who took my feet into his mouth looked to me, for a moment, like someone without much will to live, which I couldn't very well understand—he seemed otherwise such a likely candidate for happiness.

လ

There was a man in Chelsea who lived in a duplex and kept his dog (which I never saw) in the dog's own room upstairs. This man loved to smoke crack, and he wanted to blow the smoke from his mouth into mine, but he kept exhaling too soon, so I never did get high—I saw him several times. But he was just not of much interest to me. He was not much fun and he was certainly not a threat. I found him pathetic. Everything—from keeping the dog shut up in a room, to the cheap tumblers in which he served my drinks, to the sorry size and the impotence of his dick—gave me reason to pity the man. And it is not easy to fuck the mouth of a man you pity, and then to take his measly $150 while the poor dog's still locked up in its room. But I did it, and more than once.

∽

The most humiliating job I ever did was on a Saturday afternoon in the East Seventies. It was a bright, warm day, and everyone was on roller skates or a bicycle. I had been up all night on speed, and I arrived in a taxi wearing dark glasses and yawning. My agent had said the client was a young computer nerd.

Inside, the nerd (who was not young) told me that his "slave" was in San Francisco, and he hoped I would fill in for a while. I inwardly rolled my eyes, and said, Yes, sir, whatever you want. That's when he pulled open a bedside drawer full of dildoes and vibrators, and I began to wonder if I would be up for what he wanted to do. I told him that I was not prepared to have a big dildo jammed up my ass, and he said there was an enema waiting for me in the bathroom. He said I should feel free not to rush. I went into the bathroom full of consternation and hatred. I found the client repellent, and I wanted to go home. But instead I pulled my pants down and knelt on the floor to give myself an enema.

When I came out, my client was putting condoms and lubrication on the dildoes, and he was sniffing amyl nitrate, which he shared with me. He asked me if I liked to get fucked. Yes, sir, I said. I was trying hard to imagine a third man in the room—I was thinking of a porn star I often fantasized about. My client sucked my dick in a futile effort to get me aroused. When I failed to respond, he just went ahead with his plan to insert his toys into my butt. It was painful from the beginning, and I didn't know what to do. I had never considered leaving a client's apartment without being paid, and I didn't consider it then.

I forced myself to relax, and I just let the man use my body. I gave up pretending to enjoy myself, which didn't seem to bother the client at all. He handled me without concern for my pleasure. After a few minutes, I accepted the situation; and a few minutes later, I began to get off on it. There was something about *giving in* to this man I had so little to do with, who was such a complete stranger to me, and whose habits and desires were so different from my own, that finally turned me on. I forfeited the control, for a while, of my ideas of myself and of my power to make decisions, to choose one thing over another; this relaxation—or temporary demolition—of my personality was, in some kinky way, exciting. I came before the client did.

I left his apartment and went back out into the Saturday sunlight in a deep, dark haze.

ℝ

I *was* interested in a man I saw only once who lived in a beautiful apartment between Fifth and Madison in the Eighties that was furnished with old American furniture. He collected exquisite ceramic dishes and bowls all painted a glazed, shining white, in perfect condition, very old and delicate—they looked Chinese, or Japanese, though I believe that they, too, were American. The man was in his late fifties, with silver hair; he was strong look- ing and impressive, though he told me that he was melan- choly, and I believed him. He looked like someone who had always tried hard to be happy, but never was. When I arrived at his very clean home, he offered me seltzer water and tea biscuits. I knew right away that he was unusual. He was fully clothed, wearing complicated brown leather shoes laced up tight and a cravat around his neck. He did not seem to me at all like a gay man, and I

wondered if there would be any sex involved at all—he
appeared very self-reliant and free from all need. He
spoke in wonderful short paragraphs as we sat in his
kitchen sipping water and nibbling his delicious little
cookies at about seven o'clock in the evening. He was
interested to hear all about me, and I was in no hurry to
leave. He was clearly a man who enjoyed the personal ritual of seduction; the fact that he was paying me did not
seem important to him. The main thing was to be civilized and to make our time together memorable and
increasingly exciting. After nearly half an hour, he
touched my hand as it lay on the table, but only briefly
and casually—as if he didn't *long* to touch me, but had just
happened to in the course of our conversation. He asked
me my impressions of New York, and he wanted to know
if I had a boyfriend, or had had one. I told him that I had,
and told him about Tom, and about Tom's departure from
my life, with which he seemed to sympathize. He said
that he had "given up" on love, and that he paid for all the
sex he had now, and that he preferred it that way. It was
simpler this way, he said, and he had come to appreciate
simplicity. Yet he gave no sign of being ready for sex with
me, and he made me shy of initiating anything. The situation did not strike me as one free of complication.

I was turned on by him, and I wanted sex. I went to the bathroom and loitered there a while, hoping he might go to his bedroom, but when I came out he was still sitting at the kitchen table, pensive and lonely looking, with one leg crossed over the other. He looked, for a moment, like the embodiment of all the men I had ever seduced—he was intimidating and ambiguous, and the hints he gave that he wanted me were subtle and shaded. I resented his tranquil demeanor, which I thought of as dishonest. I wanted him to expose his turbulence to me; to rely on me for the succor and comfort I thought he needed. He was paying me, after all, and yet making it hard for me to do my job. I felt, for a moment, in love with him. It was all very brief and intense: he was enjoying my discomfort, but he was too kind to make it last for long. Finally he asked me to take off my clothes for him.

When I was naked, he led me to another room, where he sat on a bench and quietly told me to tilt back my head. He said, Show me your neck, which I did, standing before him. The room became very quiet, and we slowed our movements and our speech. Behind me was an enormous painting—a landscape of the West, with a stormy, brown, cloudy sky and some horses running across a dusty field. The man reached out and touched my leg, and then drew his hand up my body to my chest, then to my neck, and my face and mouth. He stood up and kissed me.

We went to his bed and lay down together. He kept his clothes on, though I unbuttoned his shirt and took off his shoes. We kissed one another for a while, and then we just lay close together, very still and passionate. I thought he had fallen asleep when I moved to get up, but he was awake. I was surprised when he paid me exactly what he owed. I had thought he would want to give me something extra.

ⲉⳁ

I must have been with a hundred men or more as an escort, but when I try to recall them, I keep thinking of the same few. I remember Bill, the regular client I have heard from recently, and I think of Jack, the sexy, rich older man with the view of the U.N. who made me feel good, and I think of the guy with the moustache in midtown with his menthol cigarettes and his neat, depressing apartment and his sad story about having just broken up, at forty-seven, with his boyfriend of six months—the only boyfriend he'd ever had. I remember the shrink in the Village and his bizarre window fetish, his passion for drugs, his lunacy and sadness and protective lack of self-awareness. I can dredge up some others. But I get the feeling that I have forgotten most of the men I met, and that I'll never remember them unless I see them again. Not that I want to remember all those lonely, mostly unattractive men; but I would like to be more adept with my memory. I would like to think I could reconstruct, with words, more of my experience of the past. Like Freud, I believe that what we have forgotten continues to do some kind of psychological work within us, and that remembering it can produce some relief from repetitive, stupid behavior.

But even the vague memories I do have of the men with whom I had sex as a hustler seem to be fading fast. The reason for this obscurity is obvious enough: I didn't want to know those men, and I don't really want to remember them. The same, unfortunately, holds for most of the men I have dated; I have been (and still am) reluctant to acknowledge my need of love and, I suppose, my lovability. I am always better in bed with a stranger than with someone I particularly like, which is a fact about myself that I regret and hope one day to reverse. Everything I believe about life persuades me that loving another person is one of the worthwhile pursuits; and yet I find it terribly hard to do. I find myself almost hoping to be disappointed by men. There is always some reason not to love the one I'm with, and to love someone else instead, or just to love my dog and my sister and my dear good friends.

Often as a hustler I brought men some satisfaction—even if it was in the form of what sometimes felt like crushing them, or squeezing them, or pounding myself against them. But I got some satisfaction from it as well. I knew what it was they were getting from me, and I know what it feels like to need that, and I understand why they need it from a stranger rather than from someone they know. Some people, if not all of us, need to be fucked hard once in a while, both physically and figuratively. We sometimes need to prove to ourselves, somehow, that we are free, in some sense, from responsibility and from civilization. Most of us are embarrassed by this need, because it seems like an expression of weakness. Certainly I am weak—to an extreme degree. I long to feel, if only for a moment, that whomever it is that is responsible for all of the chaotic business of life, it's somebody other than me. Much of every day is spent proving to the world and to ourselves that we are some-thing more than competent, that we are dependable and good at the things we do. In my experience it is not often that we relinquish all control, and that is exactly what a good hustler can help a man to do.

2 November 97

I said to L. in passing yesterday at dinner that I was a drug addict and he latched onto it and questioned me, very lovingly and lightly. I confessed and asked if he would help me find a counselor or something, which he did this morning. Now I just have to try and find the time to go. I'm nearly out of crystal, and I didn't find John at the sauna last night to buy more. I am a little nervous about running out of the stuff. I have to admit that I had a great time last night, though. I spent about five hours at the sauna, a couple of which I spent with V. B. He looked really good and we're having dinner later tonight. We had some very good sex, and then decided to split up since we both knew why we were there. The later it got the more revved up the place became until by about 4:00 A.M. I felt myself to be in quite a frenzy. Crystal, of course, can be a very sexy drug. What does all this sexiness get me? Nothing. But I have to do it, in exactly the same way that I have to write, and read, and go to work tomorrow morning, and spend more money than I should, etc. etc. etc. Everything around me, it seems, is a distraction, and either important or compelling.

12 November 97

Yesterday I got a call from Brett who wanted me to come over because he was depressed that his relationship with S. is over (again), so I went over and of course we got high. That night, there was heavy construction on the street outside, and then the neighbor across the street decided to "protest" the noise by put- ting his stereo speakers in the window and blasting disco music into the street, so we didn't get much sleep. I called Jim at the agency and he said he will give me more work.

16 November 97

I believe I broke my own record for sexual and general excess last night and this morning. I was nearly broke, and went to see Richard at his restaurant for a free meal. He was there but not working, so we proceeded to get pissed on French martinis and catch up with each other. We decided to go to the Spike and the Eagle, which were both boring, so we went to the East Village and stopped at B.'s, who seemed very distracted about S., etc. but he came out with us to the Boiler Room, which was crowded and miserable, so R. and I went to Dick's Bar, when I got paged and had to go to work at 2:30 A.M. I saw a guy called Jason on Fourteenth Street, a slightly plump but pretty well-built and nice twenty-eight year old who tipped me $50. Said he just started a new job, and asked me for a date, and I said I'd see him again for money without the agency's cut and gave him my pager number. Then I went to the sauna and waited for a room for nearly an hour, so it was 5:15 A.M. when

I got in. I left after 10 A.M. I was, of course, high on crystal, and I had a great time, though the whole experience, which lasted for most of today (beating off for hours at home until this afternoon), seems pretty ludicrous and a waste of time and uncontrollable, etc. etc. It reminds me of what somebody said on his AIDS deathbed: There was just no way I could have lived any differently—everything was inevitable and unpreventable. Which is terrifying and somehow thrilling at the same time. There is a power inside me stronger than my will or ambition or force of personality or character: it's my psychology. The trouble is, the excesses I'm prone to are so pleasurable that it's hard to think of seriously trying to give them up. This is the old suicide line again, I suppose, and betrays, I know, a deep and ill-fated depression, if not hopelessness. R. made some ballsy comments last night about my "lifestyle": said if writing is what I take most seriously then why don't I achieve more success in it? Why don't I do more of it? I was moved by his concern. He also compared our respective neuroses and said he thought he was more in control of his than I am of mine—again, he was being a good friend expressing some worry, which I was grateful for. I think, aside from a job, there are two things I need now: health insurance and a shrink. It's very hard to keep things in perspective; just how fucked up am I? Not the kind of thing I like to dwell on too much. L. just called from New Orleans.

Said he was worried about me, and about another friend of his who appears to be an alcoholic. I love L. and thank god for him.

30 November 97

Sunday evening. A long, wild weekend. R.'s new bar opened Friday night with me behind the bar. The party went on until 7, and then J., the bar back, came here for sex. I slept until 2, felt lousy, but when Charles called I agreed to meet at Film Forum for a 1968 film about a drag contest in the Cinema Verite festival, which was actually quite beautiful. We went to Julius' for a hamburger, then to Karma, where R. asked me to bartend for a while again. Went to the sauna at 3:30. At 5:30 I saw a very cute Latin boy standing up against a wall motionless. He was in a K-hole. Someone (probably the same guy that dosed him) had given me some K earlier, and it had been very nearly too much. This poor kid, though, couldn't walk at all. I stayed with him. When I asked if he wanted to be left alone, he managed to insist that I stay. I knew how he felt. Eventually we made our way to my room and as he came to appreciate the bizarre pleasure of being high on K, we had some pretty good sex. I came, and went home—in bed at 8. Up at 3:30. Victoria R. just called and wants to meet for dinner. My finances are a disaster, and everything is very strange and upset, but somehow I am not unhappy. I feel quite creative, actually—ah, to feel cre-

ative—but to BE creative, to work... Reading Sontag's pornography essay, Ivy Compton-Burnett, Vendler on Shakespeare's sonnets, the W.H. bio. for the Times, *and* Cymbeline *on Donya's recommendation.*

11 December 97

Last night was the N.Y. Observer *Xmas party at the Century. L.C. was very nice and agreed to my proposal to review Adam Phillips's new book, which J. M. just gave me a galley of. L. introduced me to Daniel M., who went out to dinner with us. I just left a message on 550-1000, on the "professional bulletin board." I need money badly.*

8.

From Nietzsche's *Daybreak*: "Thus I deny morality as I deny alchemy, that is, I deny their premises: but I do not deny that there have been alchemists who believed in these premises and acted in accordance with them.—I also deny immorality: *not* that countless people *feel* themselves to be immoral, but that there is any *true* reason so to feel. It goes without saying that I do not deny—unless I am a fool—that many actions called immoral ought to be avoided and resisted, or that many called moral ought to be done and encouraged—but I think that the one should be encouraged and the other avoided *for other reasons than hitherto.* We have to *learn to think differently*—in order at last, perhaps very late on, to attain even more: *to feel differently.*"

I have wondered if I was being immoral when I was hustling, but it never really felt like an authentic question. I was not hurting anyone apart from, perhaps, enabling some men to perpetuate an expensive bad habit. And I have never been concerned with the world's verdict on prostitutes. The world is forever making unfair judgments; people become prostitutes (and do all sorts of things) because life is hard, and life really is hard. I didn't even care very much about what the people I knew and loved thought about it. They mostly hadn't ever been prostitutes, and their opinions were therefore uninformed. (Now I gratefully acknowledge that their "opinions" were based on concern about me, and they were right to be concerned.) I suppose there was an ongoing argument within myself, but that argument never made reference to words like *morality*. *Sin* would have been closer to the kind of judgment I was inclined to make against myself, but only in a secular, somewhat ironic sense: I "sin" all the time, and have no intention of stopping.

In an essay called "Life without Principle," Henry David Thoreau wrote, "The ways in which most men get their living, that is, live, are mere makeshifts, and a shirking of the real business of life,—chiefly because they do not know, but partly because they do not mean, any better." I love that phrase, "the real business of life," and I love that for Thoreau it was obvious and given that such a thing existed. What is the real business of life? It seems to me now to be a matter of spiritual progress, and hustling was "a shirking" of it. But Thoreau's point is that so are *most* of the ways people live, and not only because we don't know any better. We seem to find it easier—at least I did, for a while—not to be seriously engaged with ourselves.

One of the aspects of hustling that I hated and eventually felt corrupted by was the willed complication many of my clients would invent because they apparently could not accept the fact that I was there with them for the money—and the way their refusal to keep things simple between us often led me to behave with them as if their version of our relationship was accurate. They *knew* that I was in it for the money, of course, but they sometimes had elaborate schemes for veiling that simple, hard fact—everything from implying that I was there to boost my ego and luxuriate in their attention; to what Bill had done: asking me at an opportune moment to tell him why I was there, and then taking my charming answer quasi-seriously. Some clients even said they did not think of me as a hustler: they just liked to "help out" young men when the young men were in need. This kind of bullshit is easy enough to dismiss, but I found it depressing to hear such remarks so often from perfectly intelligent men. It was hard to be relied upon by so many different people, if only for an hour, in an emotional, intimate way, especially by regular clients (some of whom I really was fond of, but not in the way, or to the extent, they wanted).

And, it must be said, I *wanted* to be there only for the money, whether I really was or not.

I also hated being an alcoholic and a drug addict, though I loved drinking and I loved the drugs.

The *morality* of these things—of the mendacity and the addictions—never bothered me, because I don't think of them as immoral in any public way. I would never condemn someone on moral grounds for being an ingratiating prostitute or a drug addict—or a john desperately seeking intimacy. But privately, I was too proud to accept deceitfulness, addiction, and neurasthenia as the conditions of my life. I was selling myself short, and my heart was not in it. I had real ambitions, almost at times against my will, which wouldn't permit me to complete my dissolution peacefully. Some unnameable instinct has always prodded me, gently, to find new feelings—"to feel differently." But a hustler, after a while, feels pretty much the same way all the time, and so does a drug addict. That's what habits are for: to return a person to a familiar condition. I loved the fabulous variety of men I saw as an escort because I was addicted to men, just as I liked taking any drug that came my way because I was addicted to drugs. The condition with which I was familiar was not specific to a type of man or a certain drug: I was addicted to the experience of being taken away from myself. The willful break with introspection and feeling, with my emotions and my memories and my friends, my future, and my talent—was, I knew, a dreadful mistake.

Ludwig Wittgenstein wrote in the diary he kept during the First World War: "Yesterday I was shot at. I was scared! I was afraid of death. I now have such a desire to live. And it is difficult to give up life when one enjoys it. This is precisely what 'sin' is, the unreasoning life, a false view of life. From time to time I become an *animal*. Then I can think of nothing but eating, drinking, and sleeping. Terrible! Then I suffer like an animal too, without the possibility of internal salvation. I am then at the mercy of my appetites and aversions. Then an authentic life is unthinkable."

At the front lines during one of the deadliest wars in the history of the world, Wittgenstein was "afraid of death." It had come too close, and this vision of life coming to an end gave him a "false view" of life: it gave him the illusion that life is something one might enjoy. The meanness and the violence of war, in contrast to the ease of peacetime, cast the future in a radically rosy light. And that, he says, is what "sin" is: "the unreasoning life, a false view of life." To be in the condition of "an animal" is to forfeit "the possibility of internal salvation" and the thought of "an authentic life." When he was reduced by war to the condition of an animal—able to think of nothing but eating, drinking, and sleeping—he was removed from the ongoing perfection of his mind, from the rigorous and unforgiving pruning and cleaning and streamlining of his thoughts upon which he was normally almost constantly engaged. Wittgenstein wanted to be completely unsentimental—he wanted to feel only those feelings that the world summoned and deserved. But he wanted to feel *all* of those feelings. At times during the war, he felt nothing but the pangs of hunger, thirst, fatigue, and fear. The world, he knew, was worthy of more feeling than that. And for Wittgenstein, the only sincere invitation to redemption was a complete thoughtfulness, a total reckoning with the things in the world that matter.

There were times when I was hustling when I, too, felt like an animal. I had the luxury of being concerned with sex in addition to hunger, thirst, and sleep: in fact, I worried about sex most of all. I also thought of drugs, and money. But sex was the thing that drove me into the hours of sunrise; it was the motor behind my career as a prostitute. There have been several times in my life when I have been acutely aware that I am among a species of sexual animals, and I, like Wittgenstein, have felt at those times as if salvation were a religious myth, and mental health a psychological one. Wittgenstein was more hopeful about salvation, in 1916, than I am now. But I would like to think that even a person such as I—even someone as dragged down by events as I am—can overcome the vicissitudes and the habits and the neediness we all grapple with, and live a life that is something worth caring about and persisting in. I respond to the entry in Wittgenstein's wartime diary because I know, too, that living for long without reflecting upon what I'm doing with myself is one thing—perhaps *the* thing—that can keep me from being able to honor and love my life. Prostitution was all right for a while. I knew that I was instinctively feeling very little, sometimes feeling little of anything at all—and I was interested, even glad, to know that I had that self-protective instinct. But eventually the instinct became consuming, and I didn't feel *anything* anymore, and then it was as if there were nothing inside of me to reflect upon, so I didn't think about anything except, occasionally, what was outside of me. I became an animal, and then I suffered like an animal, without the possibility of internal salvation, whatever that may be.

I have been aware for a long time that I tend toward

addictiveness, but the gradual realization that I was addicted to sex even with undesirable men was knowledge I found disturbing and finally unacceptable. There came a time when I found it impossible to separate sexual pleasure from my addiction to sexual humiliation, and it was then that I decided to write this book and to withdraw from hustling.

I find that the best way to avoid depression is to keep myself interested in things, and I am always interested in sex, even when I am interested in little else. Sex can foster, after all, both exaltation and mortification of the flesh, the achievement of both spiritual rapture and dark disgrace. Many people would agree that some pain can enhance an intense sexual situation, and there is a kind of running joke about a man's or woman's secret desire to be prostituted. While hustling rarely involves physical pain or a cliched debauchery, acquiescence to a fucked-up john's unusual requests can feel more like a degree of unwanted submission than friendly cooperation or mutual play. The bottom line for a full-time hustler is always the fact that he is working; the criteria for doing a good job are different every time, and sometimes they are more demanding than others. Some men are happy just to have a "friend" for the evening; others expect their wilder fantasies to be indulged. It's often partway through the session (when he's naked and, more often than not, high) that the hustler finds out just what will be expected of him. Compliance is a fascinating subject, with a long, sordid social history, and it figures in a complex way in everyone's psychological development. We all grapple every day with questions about whether or not we should comply with a wish, a law, a force; certainly it has been one of the themes of my life.

The one kind of morality that hustling did lead me to think about is my own private morality, by which I mean the unspoken principles that direct and inhibit my behavior—not the rules I accept intellectually or even consciously, but the bare minimum of guiding principles without which I feel lost. It is because I came up against my own minimal principles in the course of my work as a hustler and at times was unable or unwilling to grant them their efficacy that I feel able to write something about them: if I hadn't encountered my guiding principles so directly by disregarding them, I might never have known exactly what they were. Certainly while I was hustling and addicted to drugs I learned something about the seductive nature of descent: once you're falling, it is very tempting to give in to it and just finish the fall—and very hard to stop with little more than your own free will and the help of a few good friends.

I do not consider myself the least bit heroic or admirable for any of this, though I am proud of myself for having had the strength to go through it and survive it and finally to leave it—but I should never have done it, and I would think better of myself if I hadn't. Prostitution is inelegant, and I have always wanted to be an example of a certain kind of elegance—not the kind that involves money or clothes or society, but elegance resulting from the undistracted observation of one's own rigorous thinking. Thoughtlessness is the crime—or the sin—that comes before all others, and hustling requires it.

Just read the most beautiful poem. "Young Love,"
by Andrew Marvell:

> *Come, little infant, love me now,*
> *While thine unsuspected years*
> *Clear thine aged father's brow*
> *From cold jealousy and fears.*
>
> *Pretty, surely, 'twere to see*
> *By young love old time beguiled,*
> *While our sportings are as free*
> *As the nurse's with the child.*
>
> *Common beauties stay fifteen;*
> *Such as yours should swifter move,*
> *Whose fair blossoms are too green*
> *Yet for lust, but not for love.*
>
> *Love as much the snowy lamb,*
> *Or the wanton kid, does prize,*
> *As the lusty bull or ram,*
> *For his morning sacrifice.*

Now then love me: time may take
Thee before thy time away:
Of this need we'll virtue make,
And learn love before we may.

So we win of doubtful fate;
And if good she to us meant,
We that good shall antedate,
Or, if ill, that ill prevent.

Thus as kingdoms, frustrating
Other titles to their crown,
In the cradle crown their king,
So all foreign claims to drown,

So, to make all rivals vain,
Now I crown thee with my love:
Crown me with thy love again,
And we both shall monarchs prove.

The way to solve the problem you see in life is to live in a way that will make what is problematic disappear.

The fact that life is problematic shows that the shape of your life does not fit into life's mould. So you must change the way you live and, once your life does fit into the mould, what is problematic will disappear.

But don't we have the feeling that someone who sees no problem in life is blind to something important, even to the most important thing of all? Don't I feel like saying that a man like that is just living aimlessly—blindly, like a mole, and that if only he could see, he would see the problem?

Or shouldn't I say rather: a man who lives rightly won't experience the problem as sorrow, so for him it will not be a problem, but a joy rather; in other words for him it will be a bright halo round his life, not a dubious background.

—Ludwig Wittgenstein, *Culture and Value*

It's been about a year now since the last time I had sex for money. I'm no longer actively addicted to drugs and I am much less promiscuous than I used to be. When I decided I should stop taking so many drugs, I went one time to see a counselor. I told him that I used crystal meth at least twice a day. Completely unimpressed, the counselor said, So what's the problem? Is the drug working for you? And I realized that it was not—not anymore—and I stopped using it. Yoga and meditation were also helpful at the time. I continued, though, to drink a lot and to smoke pot and occasionally to use other drugs until I went to an Alcoholics Anonymous meeting on December 7, 1998. I haven't had a drink or a drug since then.

Now I have a good job working in classical music and I live with my sister and a twenty-one-year-old (straight) actor from Sweden, and a new dog, all of whom I love. My life has changed in many ways, as all lives do. When I'm not writing this book, I don't think much about the hustling I did, or the drugs or the money or the late nights in clubs, or anything else in my past: I think mostly about the present and the future, as I always have done. The past, for me, has never been a source for anything much more appealing than the present. If I am feeling unhappy, I try to plan for happiness in the future rather than dwelling on the difficulties of the past. For me it's a fact that my childhood was mostly bad, with some good moments; the ten or twelve years of my adulthood have been better. But I always expect to be happier in the future, and I try to be happy in the present. This, it seems to me, is an acceptable way to view things, though I do hope to be able one day to look back on my life (including my childhood) with more tenderness and pleasure.

I *have* thought many times about how close I came to killing myself that night when I called the suicide hot-line and cried. I wondered then and have wondered since what it would have felt like to know that I was dying—to have slit my wrists open and to feel the blood and the life draining away. I have thought about the things I would have missed out on—as I write this, I have just spent a beautiful weekend in the country and have felt very content, and have had a wonderful time with some friends and Alice, the dog. It's autumn, and in the cove across from the house I'm staying in there are two white swans and some noisy ducks, and some of the trees still have their yellow and orange leaves on them, and the sky is the same as it's always been, and these things give me great sustenance and comfort. Behind the house is an old cemetery, still used—the most recent stone is from 1996, the oldest from the eighteenth century. One small stone is for a child, three weeks old; another is for a man and a woman and their daughter, all buried and commemorated together in the same place, behind my friend's house in Connecticut. My walk in the cemetery reminds me of something another friend told me recently: he said that there is something about the fall—about the autumn air and the autumn light near the end of the day—that sometimes puts him into a terrible mood of profound depression, and he has to sit down for a minute and restore himself to the reconciliation that is normally his habit.

I think of my father, who I will probably never see again, and I vaguely wonder how I manage to get along without him. It seems, sometimes, too hard and too unjust that I should feel fatherless, that I should still feel abandoned by my dad, though he left more than twenty years ago. But then I remember that everyone has some defining problem, whether it's acknowledged or repressed, managed or circumvented, cherished or hated; and mine isn't so bad as some people's problems. I have a good life, and some wonderful friends, and right now I'm listening to a recording of a Handel opera, which I can appreciate as a great work of art. I'm able to see my problem—my sense of being unsupported—as something more than just an ugly background: it is what made me the way I am, for better or worse. This bit of intellectual good faith, this shift in attitude, gives me strength and courage and it bolsters my capacity to be happy with what I've got, which after all is plenty.

I still find it impossible most of the time to have an unskeptical, full-fledged experience of the world and of the people I get to know. I find it hard to *give in* to a wholehearted emotional moment, and I defend myself too much against people. I still *assume* positions; I remain uncommitted. I often feel as if what I am doing with my life is preparatory and meager.

I ask myself what I'm doing differently from other people, and sometimes I have to wonder if we're not all doing more or less the same thing, at least most of the time. What it is that we're doing, I'm not sure I could say.

Perhaps we're doing something different all the time, from moment to moment, always expecting to see all of the beauty and the splendor of the world and to feel something definitive sometime soon, but not just yet.